"It's been a long time since I've read a parenting book that was more enjoyable than this one. Robert Wolgemuth's helpful advice, coupled with his humor and transparency, is wonderful. Once you start reading, it will be hard to put the book down."

—GARY SMALLEY, author and founder
of the Smalley Institute

"With a five-year-old daughter, I n[...] tion. I found it in *She Calls Me Dadd[...]* me and other dads with the godly w[...]

—STEPHEN ARTERBURN, founder and chairman
of New Life Ministries

"As a clinical psychologist, I can assure you that Robert Wolgemuth's counsel is sound. As a theologian, I can affirm that his approach is solid. This book is filled with profound truth and practical ideas, and it's great fun to read. What a wonderful combination!"

—RODNEY L. COOPER, PH.D., professor,
Gordon-Conwell Theological Seminary

"One of the greatest advantages I have had in life is being well loved by my father. If he were alive today, he would agree wholeheartedly with this book. By practicing these principles, he gave my sister and me a foundation of love and confidence that nothing can shake."

—DALE HANSON BOURKE, author

"If you knew this man's daughters like I know this man's daughters, you would buy this book, read it carefully, and do exactly as it says. You would also give a copy to every man you know who's raising a daughter."

—MARK DEVRIES, president and founder
of Ministry Architects

"You want advice on raising daughters from someone who has done it. Robert Wolgemuth and his wife, Bobbie, have done it. I know their daughters, and you need look no further for examples. If you have a daughter, this is the right book for you."

—JERRY B. JENKINS, author

She Calls Me Daddy

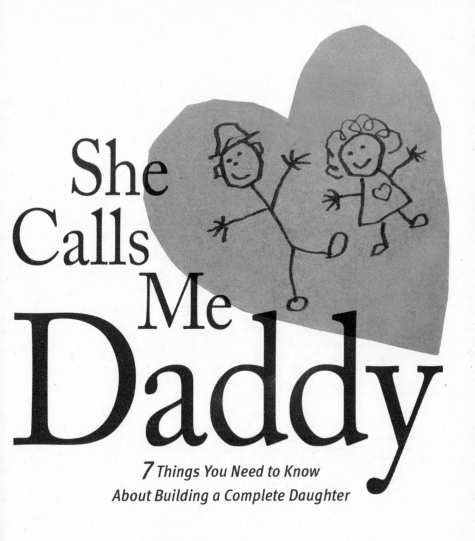

She
Calls
Me
Daddy

7 *Things You Need to Know*
About Building a Complete Daughter

ROBERT
WOLGEMUTH

Foreword by Gary and Greg Smalley

TYNDALE HOUSE PUBLISHERS, INC.
CAROL STREAM, ILLINOIS

The author is represented by the literary agency of Wolgemuth & Associates, Inc.

Editors: Larry K. Weeden and Ray Seldomridge
Cover design: THP, Ron Kaufmann
Cover photography by David Smith

Library of Congress Cataloging-in-Publication Data
Wolgemuth, Robert D.
She calls me daddy/by Robert D. Wolgemuth
cm.
ISBN-13: 978-1-58997-785-3
Fathers and daughters. 2. Parenting. 3. Fatherhood—Religious aspects—Christianity. 4. Conduct of life. I. Title
HQ756.W65   1996
307.874'2-dc20   96-2303
                              CIP

Printed in the United States of America
2   3   4   5   6/19   18   17   16   15   14

To Melissa Christine Wolgemuth Schrader
and Julie Elizabeth Wolgemuth Tassy

To Abigail Grace Schrader, Harper Corin Tassy,
and Ella Patrice Tassy

Two daughters and three granddaughters about
whom and for whom this book was written.

Your love encourages me; your affection warms me;
your relentless devotion to Jesus inspires me.

CONTENTS

Part Three
Gentlemen, We Have Our Assignments

FOREWORD

As fathers of daughters ourselves, and after counseling with hundreds if not thousands of parents, we have no doubt that girls are very different from boys. And most dads can see themselves in their sons and have some intuitive sense of what their boys need from them—the same things they sought from their own fathers.

But when it comes to girls, that's another matter. Most guys are still trying to figure out their wives—how are they to know what daughters need?

Boys often love to be tousled and teased by their dads. Girls love to be cherished. Boys can be spoken to with single words, half sentences, and grunts. Girls want their dads to talk to them in complete sentences. Boys long to live without their dad's protection. Most girls thrive with confidence when they know their dad will be there.

We fathers can so easily blow it, though. I (Gary) remember when I was driving my then-16-year-old daughter, Kari, to a basketball game to see her boyfriend play. She opened her heart to me and confided that she thought she loved him, and that they had even discussed marriage. How did I respond? Well, after I spewed my soft drink through my nose, I shouted, "I can take the love thing. But if you guys are talking about marriage, that's where I draw the line! You're only 16 years old, for crying out loud!"

As you might imagine, things only went downhill from there. And I confess that spewing soda and crushing your girl's spirit are not how I normally advise other parents to relate to their children, even in times of high stress.

Fortunately for all us dads, Robert Wolgemuth takes the mystery out of raising daughters more tenderly and effectively. As the father of two girls himself, he learned a lot of lessons that he reveals in this book, making the way a lot more clear for the rest of us.

Let us explain what particularly drew us to *She Calls Me Daddy*. One of the primary themes in our own teaching about healthy family relationships is the importance of honor, attaching high value to those you love and demonstrating it every day in how you speak to and act toward them. Happily, in a nutshell, that describes what *She Calls Me Daddy* teaches dads to do for their daughters. Its seven tools for building a daughter amount to seven great ways to honor your girl, whether she's two or 17.

Dads have always played a crucial role in the healthy development of their daughters. As Robert points out in this book, *the way you teach her and prepare her for life* will have a huge impact on whether she's ready to embrace it and live it to the fullest. *The way you treat her*—and her mother—will set her expectations for how men should treat women. *The lines of communication you establish with her* will give her a way to face the challenges and temptations with confidence and a sense of security.

In this revised edition of a now-classic book, Robert also helps us dads to cope with phenomena like texting and the Internet. We all know the modern world has become a more connected and, in many ways, a more dangerous place. But how technology is used has implications for the father-daughter relationship, too, as you'll soon discover in the following pages.

Back when this book was first published, I (Gary) said that it had been a long time since I had read a parenting title as enjoyable as this one. Since then, a lot more parenting books have been published. And you know what? The things I said then are still true. As Greg now attests as well, Robert's combination of insight, humor, and personal openness makes this a book you'll want to read. Your knowledge of how to be a great dad will grow, and it won't hurt a bit!

You've made a wise decision to pick up this book. Keep reading and you'll reap your reward. Better still, your daughter will be blessed with a smarter, better prepared, more confident, and more loving father.

Could you give your precious girl any greater gift?

—DRS. GARY AND GREG SMALLEY
Colorado Springs, Colorado

Preface

You can imagine the fun we both had the first time we read our dad's manuscript for this book. That was in 1996. We laughed out loud remembering the stories of our growing-up years.

But what was so interesting was reading the reasons behind some of the things Daddy did with us. As children, we experienced the "what" every day, but in reading this book, we learned the "why." It was really interesting to look at our dad's strategy in being our dad—kind of like seeing how a watch works after having spent a lifetime just telling time.

As kids, we had the fun of spending the night at the homes of lots of our friends. One of the things we realized was that no two families are exactly alike. Happy families come in many shapes and sizes. Some of what you're about to read will work well in your home, just as it did in ours, and some things will need to be personalized.

But simple as this might sound, there's one important thing we discovered about other families: Some of our friends were able to talk to their dads, and some weren't.

The most important thing in this book is the chapter on conversation. Of all the things our dad taught us, we're most thankful for his conversation lessons. As we grew up, our friends often asked in amazement, "You told your dad *that*?" Our ability to talk with him about our lives and how we really felt has built a bond that's the foundation of our friendship with him today.

This book includes stories about our lives when we were very young. Back then we were our daddy's little girls. Today we are his grown-up friends. And we're both married with children of our own, including daughters.

As the older sister, I (Missy) was the first to walk down the aisle in 1994.[1] In February 1996, our daughter, Abby, was born. Because of this book, my husband, Jon, had a quick guide . . . and owner's manual. Of course, he had known about *She Calls Me Daddy* before Abby was born, but now he had a reason to read it. And he did.

As the second daughter, I (Julie) got married in July 1999. In February of 2002, our first daughter, Harper, was born. Sixteen months later her sister, Ella, came along.

Even though Jon and Christopher are different men and have fathered their daughters in different ways than he fathered us, they took much of our daddy's advice, which you'll read about in the introduction.

You'll probably disagree with some of what you'll read in this book. That's to be expected, and of course that's okay. If, however, in your disagreement, this book raises some good questions, helping you make progress toward your own effective parenting, then so much the better.

There are two things our husbands have done just as our dad did. First, they talked to their daughters about purity. At the end of chapter 3, Dad describes how he gave us something special that he later presented to our husbands at our wedding receptions. I (Missy) received "the key to my heart" on a necklace, and Dad gave me (Julie) a promise ring.

Second, Daddy loved our mom more than he loved us. He knew that this would represent security to us, even when we were very young and didn't fully understand how loving our mom would impact us. He talks about this in chapter 5.

We really hope this book is helpful to you and your daughter(s), just as its principles were to us.

And thanks, Daddy, for encouraging us to fall in love with our husbands . . . and for celebrating the fact that, just as you love our mom even more than you love us, we love Jon and Christopher even more than we love you . . . and that's a lot.

—MISSY WOLGEMUTH SCHRADER
and JULIE WOLGEMUTH TASSY

Introduction

Most writers wait until their manuscript is finished before they write the introduction to the book. I know this is counterintuitive—like saying hello to someone you're on the verge of leaving. But when you think about it, a book introduction is a summary of what you're about to read and, until the thing is finished, even the person doing the writing isn't certain of all the twists and turns.

So I've chosen to break tradition and write this for what it really is—an introduction.

In 1995, after a long conversation with my wife, Bobbie, I decided to try something I had never tried before—namely, write a book. I knew what the book was going to be about: raising daughters. And I knew which readers I had in mind: dads. Men who knew nothing from their own experience about what they were doing.

So *She Calls Me Daddy* was written. And published.

At the time, our daughter Missy was 25 and Julie was 22. They were both out of college. Missy was married to Jon Schrader. Julie was working for my company as our CFO and writing songs. Her music company was called Manor Music . . . man or music, get it?

But within two and a half years and in God's sweet providence, Christopher Tassy came along, and she had found her life's partner.

In publishing parlance, *She Calls Me Daddy* became a best seller, launching what I had never could have expected . . . amazingly more books. (The lowest grade I received in high school was from Miss Felgar in literature.) And these books have been wonderfully fulfilling to write. But, as you might imagine, the first will always be very special.

A few years ago, I bumped into my editor, Larry Weeden, at a book convention. He asked if I would be interested in updating *She Calls Me Daddy*. In his gentle way, Larry reminded me that in the years since 1996, the world had undergone dramatic changes. (Larry is one very smart man.) And the impact that these changes have had on parenting is undeniable. For example, the book made no mention of the power of electronics. When it was written, I had never used the word *texting*, and I could not have imagined actually taking photographs with my phone or posting them on such a thing as "Facebook" so literally thousands of people could see them instantly. Larry was right; a lot had changed.

So I talked it over with Bobbie. She thought it would be a good idea to ask Missy and Julie. They suggested that I talk it over with their husbands, Jon and Christopher, also fathers of daughters.

As it turns out, there was unanimous enthusiasm for updating the book. Not only that, there was an offer from all of the above to pitch in and help.

So everyone in the family took a copy of the original, read through it carefully, and made notes. Then on a special weekend at the Ballantyne Hotel in Charlotte, we[1] met and talked through the book, paragraph by paragraph, suggesting changes that needed to be made. Some material needed to be added. Tragically, some had to retire! We wrestled through the concepts and beefed up the faith chapter.

What you have here is the result of this adventure. It's all our hope that you find this book helpful and encouraging . . . and challenging. These days, the task of being a daughter, and raising a complete daughter, is a big one.

⌒

Bobbie and I both had the luxury of growing up in solid Christian homes. Most of our family-of-origin memories are good. Some of what we did with our girls was similar to what we had seen our parents do, and some of it was quite different. We established our own "family normals."

By the time I wrote *She Calls Me Daddy*, I had been professionally connected to the publishing industry for more than 20 years, so we were surrounded by helpful articles and books, and some of what we did as parents came from them. We also had the privilege of attending many helpful seminars and workshops.

Although some of the information in this book did come from our parents, books, and helpful experts, a great deal of our inspiration during those 25 years came from the Bible. Bobbie is a voracious reader of the Scriptures, and nearly every morning during our daughters' growing-up years (and ever since), she sat on her most comfortable chair with a Bible and a journal. My undergraduate degree was in Bible, and since 1969, I have taught Sunday school. The Bible is my primary resource.

So, armed with the truth of God's Word, Bobbie and I prayed a simple parenting prayer: "Lord, You've entrusted us with these girls. Now, since we're total amateurs, please help us raise them as You would have us raise them. And, while You're at it, please fill us with Your Spirit too."

I suppose it's inevitable that parts of this book will appear to some as Wolgemuth home movies. "Aw, come on, please . . . take a look at just a *few* more pictures from our summer trip to the Grand Canyon!" Frankly, I'm embarrassed at the thought. What we have is a gift from God, including the girls and our relationships with them. Much of what we've learned has come from our failures. In other words, if it sounds as though I have some things figured out, it's only because I made enough mistakes to know what doesn't work. I'm not showing off, believe me. After all, Bobbie and I were thrust into this parenting thing pretty quickly. Bobbie was 21 when Missy was born, and I was 23. In many ways, we were just children ourselves.

ABOUT THIS BOOK

Although many of the stories and illustrations in this book refer to me in the singular, I assure you that this job of raising girls has been a partnership. Not only has Bobbie been an essential ally in the process, but she has also been a reservoir of sound information and advice. Where else could I get inside information about raising a woman than from a woman? And Bobbie has helped me to appreciate that, even in raising daughters, my intentional participation is critical. Parenting is a team sport.

Instead of tracing our experiences and the lessons we've learned in chronological order, this book will take you through seven major themes: protection, conversation, affection, discipline, laughter, faith, and conduct.

Because I'm a hopeless tinkerer—a weekend warrior—a construction theme runs through what you're about to read. When I'm in the middle of a project and have to run to the store for more supplies, I grab a piece of scrap wood or a broken corner of drywall and make a list using the pencil that's usually tucked above my right ear. I do this because if I don't write it down, I'll forget. Don't smile at me. You forget too. So, at the end of chapters 2 through 10—which includes the seven theme chapters—I've summarized the material in a "Builder's Checklist" so you can more easily recall the main points.

You'll find many things in this book that are helpful for raising sons, too, but I've especially aimed these chapters at dads and daughters. According to some of my friends who have sons, there really is a difference. And raising girls is what I know.

Even though my fathering situation has been a traditional one—mom and dad at home with their own natural children—this book closes with an afterword that addresses the unique needs and concerns of dads in special situations. Thanks to friends who are divorced, single, or blended-family dads, I've been helped to understand some important differences in these environments.

After you read this book, if you decide to give it to someone else to read—or buy another copy—find a dad with a *young* daughter. The earlier a dad starts thinking through these principles, the better his chances will be of succeeding. Yet, I think they'll prove helpful to any dad, regardless of his daughter's age.

My hope and prayer is that God will give you wisdom as you take on this huge and wonderful task of building a girl. Not just any girl. *Your* daughter.

—Dr. Robert Wolgemuth
Orlando, Florida

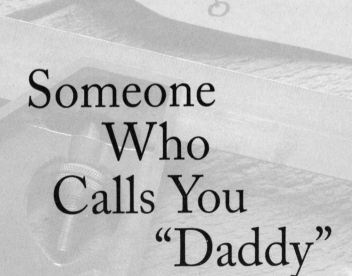

PART ONE

Someone Who Calls You "Daddy"

What's a Nice Guy Like You Doing in a Book Like This?

*If I sat here for three or four weeks, I could
not adequately describe just how important
the father-daughter relationship is.*
—Dr. James Dobson

"Are you awake?"

It had been almost an hour since we had gone to bed, but I sensed that my wife, Bobbie, hadn't dozed off either, so I broke the silence with the question.

"Uh-huh," came her quiet reply.

Then, trying not to sound too worried, I asked if she thought it was about time for us to hear our 15-year-old daughter walking through the front door. "When did Missy say she would be home?" I asked, mustering all the confidence I could to keep my voice from quavering.

"Around eleven," Bobbie returned, her voice sounding strong and sure. She had decided to put on the same act.

We lay there for a few more minutes, neither of us speaking. Before asking the question, I had checked my nightstand clock. It was 11:25. I knew Missy was late—not a normal thing for her. More silence.

"Maybe we ought to make a call to see if we can find her," I finally said, losing most of my on-top-of-it tone of voice.

In a flash, Bobbie's nightstand lamp was on, and she was dialing. A sleepy youth pastor's wife finally picked up the phone. "Susan, this is Bobbie Wolgemuth, and I'm sorry to call you so late, but have Missy and David left your house?"

Although I couldn't hear Susan's answer, I could tell by Bobbie's tone as the conversation continued that the kids had left a long time before, with plenty of time to be home by now.

"Where's Missy?" Bobbie said as she hung up the phone, making no attempt to hide her frustration and fear.

Our daughter and her friend David had been at Mark and Susan's for a Sunday night Bible study. David was a 17-year-old boy who was like a brother to Missy and a son to us. A welcome "member" of our family, David would come and go from our house without ever knocking on the door. Our TV was his TV. Our refrigerator was his refrigerator. We liked that.

But tonight, David was keeping me from going to sleep, and I wanted to know why.

We waited. Eleven forty-five, no Missy. Midnight, no Missy. Ten after twelve …

"I'm getting up," I finally announced. "I'm going downstairs to wait."

Bobbie said nothing. She was either praying for Missy or planning David's caning in the mall parking lot.

By the time I made it to the front door, David's car was turning into our driveway, his headlights sweeping across the front of our house. "Finally," I said loud enough for Bobbie to hear me upstairs. "She's home."

Instead of trudging back up the stairs to bed, I thought I'd wait for Missy to get inside so I could ask her to explain where she had been and why she hadn't called.

David's car came to a stop, the headlights went out, the engine went quiet, and both David and Missy launched from each side of the car and came bounding up the walk to the front door.

Standing there in nothing but my snow-white Jockey shorts, I quickly came to two realizations: (1) There was no time to dash up the stairs without being seen, and (2) if I stepped around the corner into the living room, no one would ever see me in that condition. In the next room, I found a good shadowed spot.

The front door opened, and Missy came in with David right on her heels. *What's going on?* I wondered. *Don't these kids know what time it is?*

Missy scrambled up the stairs to get something, leaving David standing just inside the front door. For what seemed like a minute or two, he stood there, not having any idea that Missy's dad was just around the corner.

Then it happened. David began to move, and as he did, he started quietly humming. I could tell by the growing sound of the "music" that he was shuffling toward the living room.

I panicked, my mind dropping into overdrive. *If I tuck myself into the shadow next to the piano, he'll never see me.* I was proud of myself for thinking so quickly at that time of the night.

David walked to the doorway into the living room and stopped. Continuing to hum, he scanned the darkness. I felt like a fugitive hiding from the long arm of the law . . . in my own house. I could clearly see him. He could not see me.

Unfortunately, David began to move again, coming right toward the piano where I was standing.

By the time he finally saw me, this unsuspecting, red-headed, 17-year-old boy was about 10 inches away. There he stood, Mr. All-Conference-Student-Leader-and-Everyone's-Favorite-Teenage-Boy. And there I stood, Tarzan of the Living Room.

"Hello, David," I said casually, as though I had bumped into him at a school function. "What are you doing here?"

The boy gasped, quickly sucking in just enough air to keep from collapsing. His body froze, but in the darkness, I could see his eyes moving up and down, scanning my terrific outfit.

At that moment, Missy burst into the living room. A stuffed animal the kids at church passed around like a mascot—a green snake named "Cecil"—was tucked under her arm.

"Dad," she exclaimed, "what are *you* doing here?"

Good question.

What Are You Doing Here?

Whatever the reason you have this book in your hand, you're probably a dad with a daughter and you *are* here. Maybe you're a brand-new father of a baby girl, and you want to find out what you're in for. Or perhaps your daughter has been around for a few years, and although you think you're doing a pretty good job as the daddy, you'd like some help. It could be that your daughter is just about to step across the threshold into womanhood, and you're a little nervous.

> *Being the father of a girl can be a journey into the great unknown, and it makes no sense to go it alone.*

Whatever the reason, I'm glad you're here. Being the father of a girl can be a journey into the great unknown, and it makes no sense to go it alone especially when you don't need to. You've spent your whole life as a male, so you know that if this were a son, you could give him a pointer or two from your own experience as he moves through his growing-up years. But this is a girl, and there are two things you know for sure: (1) She's your responsibility, and (2) you have no personal experience that will help you.

ARTIST'S RENDERING OF THE FINISHED PROJECT

During my years in sales, I visited many corporate lobbies. While waiting for an appointment, I rarely sat down. Sitting made me even more nervous than I was already. This was usually a source of frustration for the receptionist, who would repeatedly order me to sit by gently "inviting" me to take a seat.

"Can I get you something?" she would ask.

"No, thank you," I'd say without sitting down.

"Are you sure I can't get you something?"

"Thank you. I'm sure."

Often, I'd slowly circle around those lovely waiting areas looking at things on the wall. Sometimes there were paintings, or plaques of recognition awarded to this company. Sometimes I would see a framed and colorful illustration—an artist's rendering—of the corporation's next building expansion. It was a new wing on the existing building or a whole new building. In either case, given my love for construction, I would be fascinated with those glimpses into the future, studying every detail. Sometimes I'd study the cars that the architects had painted in the pretend parking lots, trying to see if I could identify the models.

Let's say that once the corporation found enough capital to proceed with their new building and all the bids were in, Cousin Larry's Construction Company got the project. If Cousin Larry was as smart as everyone said he was, he would have asked for that drawing to be hung in a place where his employees and subcontractors could see it every day. Maybe in the construction trailer. It would have been a great help to Larry and his people if they could begin—and continue—working on this project, focusing not on the necessary work and details of any complex construction assignment but on the *finished* product—the beautiful results.

The greatest challenge you'll face as the father of a daughter is to keep from being distracted by the day-to-day stuff—the little duties and challenges and frustrations that can easily capture a dad's full-time attention. Instead, I'm encouraging you to do what Cousin Larry did. Keep a picture in your mind of what it is you're building here: a healthy, poised, confident, balanced, and happy woman—a complete daughter who will someday be counted among your closest friends. Begin—and continue—building with the end in mind.

This book will help you do that.

The Project of a Lifetime

Don't you love Saturday mornings? You go to bed late Friday night, knowing you can sleep in as long as you want because the weekend has arrived. But suppose one particular Saturday morning, something's wrong. You're lying in bed wide awake, and there's no going back to sleep.

The dawning sun hasn't even squeezed through the bedroom blinds. You glance at the digital clock on your nightstand: 6:11! *So why is it so tough to wake up on a weekday when I* have *to get up*, you think, *but now that I can sleep as late as I want to, I'm lying here wide awake?*

The answer is simple. You've got a project. You've been looking forward to starting it for a long time. It's going to take a stack of pressure-treated wood, which was delivered this week. You've been to Home Depot (or whatever the huge, buy-every-possible-building-supply-you-could-ever-need-under-one-roof warehouse store is called where you live) and loaded up. *Beep.* "Someone in Lumber dial 3-4-4." The guy in building supplies with the orange canvas bib that said, "Hello, my name is Dave. Can I help you?" was quite that—helpful. Now you've got your galvanized nails and bolts, a new extra-long drill bit, and several bags of premixed concrete.

You can hardly wait to get started.

Because your wife *doesn't* have a construction project this morning, she is still sleeping. You try to make very little noise. Quietly pulling on a pair of old jeans and crawling into your favorite sweatshirt, you slip out your bedroom door, tiptoe down the hallway so you don't wake the baby, then head down the stairs and into the garage, where everything is waiting.

You and your wife have been talking for a long time about building a deck on the back of the house. You've walked around your backyard many times, surveying the site. You've even stood where the deck will be, envisioning your new view when it's done. And you have one of those oversized, chrome propane gas grills on layaway, waiting for its new home.

Your neighbors have heard all about this deck, and frankly, they're hoping it looks great so they can (have you help them) build one, too.

Projects are terrific.

THIS LITTLE GIRL OF OURS

Because you're reading this book, you've probably stood at your wife's hospital bedside and looked into the squinting, ruddy face of a brand-new baby girl. Not, of course, just any baby girl, but *your* baby girl.

You know the awe, the thrill of realizing she's yours. This is a remarkable other-world sensation, isn't it?

My son-in-law Christopher, a grandson of the country of Haiti, has tawny skin and jet black eyes. His wife, our Julie, has dark brown eyes, so there was no doubt that their first child's eyes would lean toward ebony. The chances for a blue-eyed infant were zero.

A guest-with-daddy-privileges in the delivery room, Christopher stood where he could witness the baby's introduction to the world. Doctors and nurses scurried about. Exhausted from hours of hard labor, Julie pushed.

"Suddenly I saw the baby's face," Christopher told me later. "Her eyes were wide open." He paused and gathered his composure. "Dad," he told me that morning, "she was looking right at me. It was like those eyes were saying, 'So you're the guy?'"

Many years later, the feeling of that moment is still etched in Christopher's memory. "I was suddenly a dad."

For Christopher, even though this happened many years ago, the joy and sobriety of the sight of those eyes looking right at him is still very fresh. Handing him a large, shiny, and very clean pair of scissors, the doctor asked Christopher to cut the umbilical cord.[1] He squeezed, and the cord was severed. Until this instant, the baby had literally been connected to her mother. Miraculously, helping to shape little Harper's character would now be his responsibility.

> *This is going to be the most unbelievable project you've ever tackled.*

You have your own story, don't you? Go back to that moment in your memory right now. Are you there?

What year was it? What was the name of the hospital? Do you remember the name of your wife's doctor? What time of year was it? What time of day? How long had your wife been in labor? Were you tired? Was your wife tired? (I'm kidding.)

Okay, are you standing there? It's an amazing moment—an absolutely breathtaking, speechless moment. You don't remember ever feeling such wonder.

Perhaps you're thinking, *Is this really happening to me? Is this little person actually mine? When am I going to be able to take her home? What will I do with her when we get home? She looks so fragile. If I pick her up, will she break? I can barely handle myself . . . and my marriage . . . now this!*

What I want you to do is to see yourself looking at that baby, just as you stood in your backyard imagining the deck you were about to build. This is going to be the most unbelievable project you've ever tackled. You're responsible to help "build" this little girl into a woman.

Sure, there are others who *could* do it, but you're the dad, and in spite of how you feel at the moment, no one is more qualified than you.

And just like that Saturday morning when you couldn't sleep in, suddenly it's time to get excited about this project—very excited. In fact, I'll make you a promise: This project will give you more satisfaction than any old wooden deck possibly could.

And What About Tomorrow?

Now we're going on another journey. This one's into the future.

Your "little" girl has never looked more angelic than she does at this moment. The radiance of her face almost seems to be throwing off light. Her dress is the purest white you think you've ever seen.[2]

The two of you are standing in front of closed double doors, and she has her arm gently tucked under yours. The organist begins playing, the doors open, and you and your daughter are slowly walking down the center aisle of a familiar place, your home church. You can feel your heart pounding in your temples. The people are standing. You look left and right into the faces of well-wishers. Extended family. Lifetime friends. You have never been more proud. You're having one of those epiphanies where you can almost stand back and watch yourself. You don't remember having the bottom of your feet tingle before, but this is actually happening. It's an overwhelming and awesome experience.

The walk to the front of the sanctuary has ended. You stand silently while the organist finishes the processional.

Except for the tingling in your feet, your whole body is numb, almost trancelike. You've been a guest at so many of these things and seen other dads standing with the bride, but you never expected it to be quite like this.

The minister has finished his opening remarks. You know he's getting close to asking you the big question. You're just about to place your girl into someone else's care for the rest of her life. For a split second, you panic.

What's my line? What's my cue? What am I supposed to say? Can someone please help me? Your mind screams for the words.

But just as you practiced the night before, when the minister says, "Who gives this woman to be married to this man?" you calmly speak the words that close the deal: "Her mother and I do."

You gently take her hand from your arm, place it into the minister's hand, and quietly sit down.

In the spring of 1994, Bobbie and I attended a very formal wedding. Brittany, one of our daughter's best friends, was getting married. The church was impeccably decorated with flowers and packed from aisle to aisle with well-dressed guests. The strains of the organ swelled as the bride and her father walked to the front of the church. Everyone stood. It was one of those lump-in-your-throat moments.

As the majestic processional ended, the robed and somber minister opened a small, black book and read a few appropriate and, of course, formal remarks. His booming voice filled the sanctuary.

When he was finished, he invited the congregation to be seated. We obeyed.

Then, suddenly and without warning, the minister broke character. It was almost as though he had wakened from a spell. This big-city-seminary-trained, austere man of the cloth looked up from his little book and straight into the face of the bride's father. "Well, Johnny," he boomed, "I guess this is the end of the road."

Some of the guests snickered. Some laughed out loud. Fathers with unmarried daughters, including me, audibly gasped. I don't remember anything else about that ceremony.

Well, my fathering friend, someday when you take your own daughter for the short walk down that aisle, it *will be* the end of the road for you, too.

For some dads, helping a daughter pack all her grown-up things into a U-Haul and watching her drive off to seek her fortune will be that "walk down the aisle." In either case, they're setting their daughters free. What they've done to prepare them for that moment is finished.

This book will help you get ready for that moment.

YOU'RE WHAT?

I fell into this fathering thing unexpectedly. I know how it happened; I just wasn't prepared.

It was February 1971, just 11 months after our wedding. Bobbie and I were driving to Minneapolis from our home in Chicago to attend a business convention. I was glad Bobbie was able to come with me on this trip, but she seemed unusually tired as our car headed north into the bitter-cold night.

I battled high winds and slippery highways. This was long before mandatory seat belt laws, and Bobbie spent most of the trip stretched out on the backseat, only occasionally waking to make sure I was okay. I scanned the radio dial, unsuccessfully trying to find something more interesting than hog futures.

I listened to Bobbie's irregular breathing. I could tell this was more than just being extra tired. Bobbie wasn't feeling well.

I sure hope it's not the flu, I worried.

The day after we arrived in the Twin Cities, still not feeling right, she whispered her own diagnosis to me. Too overwhelmed to hear herself say the words above a whisper, she said softly, "Honey, I think I'm pregnant."

The words took my breath away. I couldn't believe it.

I was on the staff of a youth ministry, and she was a full-time college student. Because we lived on donations and a part-time job that Bobbie had working for the school librarian, our money barely lasted a month at a time.

"What are we going to do?" she asked repeatedly during the next few days. The swirling reality of this responsibility began to sink in.

What *were* we going to do?

After our return to Chicago, Bobbie made an appointment with her doctor. She wanted to be sure. I went along for support.

The only man sitting in the waiting room, I remember surveying the women seated in the chairs around the perimeter of the room. They were at varying stages of readiness. Most were chatting openly with their neighbors about intimate and graphic details of physiological changes and surprises. I could feel the color draining from my face. It was all I could do to hang on.

And then I saw her. My wife of less than one year walked from the hallway through the door and into the waiting room where I sat. Our eyes locked immediately. Hers welled up with tears. So did mine. She nodded ever so slightly. She reminded me of an angel.

Pregnant on Purpose!

Most of our friends were married couples three or four years older than us. All of them had determined they were going to wait until they could "afford" children. And I guess, without actually discussing it, that's where we were headed too.

We suspected that these friends, once they learned we were expecting a baby, would be shocked. "You're pregnant? What happened? Surely this must be a big surprise!"

So before any of those comments came our way, Bobbie and I sat down to talk it over.

"You know," I remember saying, "even though this really is a total shock, let's tell everyone this pregnancy was planned. We can't imagine how things are going to work out, but God has obviously blessed us with this baby, so between you and me, let's just rest in the fact that it was God's plan. Let's tell everyone that this baby was exactly what we had in mind."

Bobbie agreed. What else would we say about God's plan? So that's what we decided to do.

And sure enough, friends asked. Some were diplomatic. Subtle. "Hmmm, what an interesting time in your lives to start a family." Others were really direct: "You're what?"

Even more surprising than the pregnancy itself was our confident response. I can still see them shaking their heads in disbelief.

The closer we got to delivery day, the more excited we became. The summer of 1971 was unusually warm and humid, even for Chicago. So we bought a used air-conditioning unit; a friend and I hoisted the heavy thing into the living room window. Bobbie spent most of her last months of pregnancy standing directly in front of its coldest output. I watched as her belly swelled, clearly thankful to be a man.

In mid-September, our little girl was born.

WHAT DID I KNOW ABOUT GIRLS?

I was disappointed. I'll admit it.

Though I didn't whisper a word of this to Bobbie at the time, I really had wanted a boy—a son who would help me with building projects; a son I could tussle with on the living room floor; a son who, by some miraculous quirk of genetic fate, would be the athlete I never was. But it wasn't to be.

In three days, we brought our baby home from the hospital. And in no time, we discovered we were about to go through the adjustment of our lives. That adjustment made the passage from being single to getting married look like nothing at all.

But there was no turning back. Try as we might to return to full nights of sleep and lazy, selfishly designed evenings, they were gone. Forever.

Who Are You, Little Girl?
What's to Become of You?

Soon after Missy came home to live with us, I learned to do diapers. Don't smile at me. You had to do the same.

This was before Pampers, so I had to get comfortable scraping the treasure off the cloth diaper into the toilet while safely managing the gag reflex. There were Desitin and baby powder, but, in 1971, no little tabs to cinch the thing closed. Learning to use a safety pin the size of a wrench without sticking her was up there on the scale of difficulty with learning to do crown molding without any gaps. I actually did pretty well with this.

In no time I forgot the nonsense about the boy. This little person was capturing my heart. I couldn't wait to get home from work to look at her and hold her.

Late one afternoon, I was lying on the carpeted floor of our living room, cuddled next to baby Missy. She was on her tummy, a clean cloth diaper under her head, with her face turned toward me. I studied her tiny features—her velvety skin, little turned-up nose, and rosebud mouth.

We talked.

"Do you know who you are, little girl?" I asked. "You're Missy, and I'm your daddy. Do you know how glad I am that you came to live at our house? Do you know how much I love you?"

Occasionally her eyes would squint open, trying to focus.

I raised up enough to lean over and kiss her soft cheek. My hand rested on her back, softly patting. Drool trickled out of the corner of her mouth.

As though it were yesterday, I can remember the breathtaking feeling in my soul, not unlike the moment a roller coaster begins its descent.

"This little girl is my responsibility," I breathed out loud. "I'm her daddy, the only one she'll ever have."

The feeling was overwhelming, but not a frustrated or fearful kind of overwhelmed. I felt resolved. Committed. Ready to tackle the obstacles that would surely lie ahead.

I remember lying there next to this baby person and whispering, "I'll *be* your daddy, little girl. You can count on me. I can do this. I know I can."

And in that moment I added a prayer. "God, please help me."

My project had begun.

Hanging in There

Sure, I Can Finish This Today

> *That which we persist in doing becomes
> easier—not that the nature of the task has
> changed, but our ability to do has increased.*
> —Ralph Waldo Emerson

It's a lot easier for me to start a project than to finish one. Why? Because I am, at the core of my being, a quitter. I suspected this about myself during my growing-up years. Assembling plastic model airplanes and boats, I can remember getting about halfway in and suddenly thinking of something more fun. This propensity for quitting came into clear focus during the summer of 1968.

Without really thinking it through, along with 39 friends who apparently didn't think it through either, I ventured out on a bicycle trip that started in San Francisco. We were headed for New York City. Between those two cities, I was ready to quit many times, and only pride and the peer pressure of the group kept me from doing just that.

Our first day on the road started like some kind of party. The press was there taking photos of our group, with the Golden Gate Bridge providing a spectacular backdrop. As our police motorcycle escort whisked us through the cities of San Francisco and Oakland, we idealistic college men felt like Olympic marathoners, entering the stadium for the final two laps. Because the news had told locals about our adventure, crowds gathered on the sidewalks—children waved and cheered, dogs barked, men stood at attention with their hands over their hearts, and women softly cried and waved white handkerchiefs. (All this is true except for the part about the men and women.)

Unfortunately, unlike marathoners at the end of their run, our trip was just beginning. We had thousands of miles to go!

On our way to Walnut Creek, directly out of Oakland, we headed north on St. Mary's Road—the county tricked us into using this road by giving it a gentle, pious-sounding name. In only a few miles, we went from sea level to an altitude of almost 2,000 feet. I thought I was going to die. My greatest disappointment was that I didn't.

Riding one of the first versions of a 10-speed bike, I had, before this day, spent little time in first gear. The few times I had tried it, it seemed as if my feet were traveling faster than the wheels were turning. It was so easy to pedal that I almost fell off the bike.

But on this afternoon—the whole afternoon—we were in first gear. I kept checking to see if my tires were flat. *This must be what it's like to jog in waist-deep molasses*, I thought. My legs were on fire, and my chest felt as though it were about to burst.

I decided that starting this trek had been great fun, but I really didn't want to finish it. Realizing I had 41 more days to go and that I had made the mistake of a lifetime, I decided to cash it in. If I had found someone to swap with, I would have traded my bike for a one-way bus ticket to Chicago in a second. No question about it. Unfortunately, I found no one to make the trade.

Forty-two days later, I stood on the easternmost banks of New York Harbor, staring at Lady Liberty. For every single day of the previous six weeks, I had peddled a 28-pound Schwinn Super Sport from dawn to dusk. No days off. No relief for my aching legs or terminally bruised rear end. No sleeping in a bed or eating my mother's cooking.

But, amazingly, this quitter had made it.

There was the day of riding on Highway 160, between Cortez and Durango, Colorado, suffering from the worst case of diarrhea I had ever experienced. In spite of having been on the road for almost two weeks, I lost six *more* pounds. That day. The grind in my stomach ached so badly that I spent most of the day with tears on my face. I was miserable. I wanted desperately to quit. But I didn't.

And when I didn't, I thought, *Hey, I didn't quit. I wanted to quit. I schemed of how I could talk my way out of being too embarrassed by quitting, but I didn't do it. I didn't quit.*

In Missouri, Kenny Parks thought he'd tighten the quick-release hub on his front wheel with his foot, but instead he stuck his low-cut black Converse Chuck Taylor All-Star sneaker directly into the spokes. Unfortunately, I was riding about 10 inches behind him, and in a moment we were both tumbling down the asphalt—bicycle, Kenny, bicycle, me, bicycle, Kenny, bicycle, me, and so on.

When the tumbling finished, I lay there on Highway 65, just west of Marshall, and wanted to quit again. The palms of my hands were skinned and bleeding. My legs were cut and scraped. I had had enough of this trip. I wanted to quit, but I didn't.

And when I didn't, I thought, *Hey, I didn't quit. I wanted to quit. My bleeding and bruised body wanted to quit, but I told it not to quit, and it obeyed.*

Two weeks later, a few miles east of Morristown, New Jersey, on Highway 24, it happened again. This time Kenny Parks was showing off and bounced his bike into a concrete curb. Instantly his wheel snapped into a twisted coil, and he was down. Because he was a great rider, I was right behind him, drafting. The tumble in Missouri was a distant memory. So I was again just a few inches behind him. In a split second, we were both tumbling down the asphalt. Bicycle, Kenny, bicycle, me, Kenny . . . all over again.

And even though we were less than a hundred miles from the East Coast, I wanted to quit. What I *had* done was fairly significant.

After all, I had made it all the way to New Jersey. I wasn't completely finished, but I was *almost* finished. Close enough.

I'd had enough of this bicycle trip—and Kenny Parks. I wanted to quit, but I didn't. And when I didn't, I thought, *Hey, I didn't quit. I wanted to quit, but I didn't. I may be a quitter by nature, but that doesn't mean I have to quit.*

The Peril of Underestimation

I'm not sure why, but in addition to being a quitter by nature, I'm a bad guesser—especially when it comes to estimating when I'm going to be able to finish something. It can be anything—a trip to the grocery store, a call to a customer or client, or a building project. Countless times, I've heard myself promising Bobbie, "I'll be finished today. Tomorrow for sure."

> *Things usually do take longer than planned—sometimes a lot longer.*

I've really meant it, too. I really thought I was going to finish. I wasn't lying—at least not intentionally. Don't I get some credit for not intending to lie? I really thought I could finish something before the sun went down, but it took me many additional days—or weeks or months.

Over the years, I've learned I have a lot of company as a quitter. And maybe that's because things usually do take longer than planned—sometimes *a lot* longer. We get all fired up in the beginning, but the fire fades. It's not the fun we thought it was going to be. *This feels an awful lot like work.*

Please Read This Carefully

You may be wondering where I'm going with all this stuff, but please stay with me. What follows may be the most important part of this book.

When your daughter was born, you were euphoric. You thought, *I'm a daddy. Being a daddy is so cool.* You even told your friends how much fun you were having.

But soon after your little girl came to live with you, your "legs" began to ache, your "palms" were bleeding and sore. You found yourself wondering if you could take this one back. You turned your girl over, hoping to see "Refundable" or "Return for Deposit" stamped somewhere. No such luck.

This one was a keeper. There was no turning back.

Now I want you to admit something. In fact, I want you to say it out loud. Yes, in spite of sounding like your mother, I want you to say it out loud this minute. Don't mumble the words; speak them forcefully. Ready? Here they are:

> *"I'd rather start a project than finish it."*

Did you say that? Congratulations if you did.

If you didn't say those words out loud, go back and try again.

Did you do it?

Good for you.

Why did I ask you to do this? Because if you're like me—and you probably are in this respect—you're a quitter to the core. Rather than see a project through to completion, you'd prefer to start it and then, when it stops being fun, walk away. And I'm talking about totally completing something—all-the-scraps-of-wood-and-stuff-tossed-in-the-trash-and-tools-put-away completed.

But now that you've got this little girl living in your house, it's your job to help "build" her. You can't quit.

When she cries in the night—all night—for the fifth night in a row, you can't quit. When she rides her tricycle too close to your car and lays down a razor-fine scrape on the driver's side door, you can't quit. When she's older and you try every bribe imaginable to get her to pick up after herself, and she just can't seem to do it, you can't quit.

When you've specifically told her that she cannot use her electronics until she finishes her homework, and she disobeys, you can't quit. When her grades drop because she's having so much fun (see above reference to electronics), you can't quit.

What's worse, building this girl is a project that's going to take a long, long time. In most cases, it will take about 20 years to finish. Your mileage may vary, depending on conditions. But don't quit. Don't let her get potty trained and then let her go. You're not finished yet.

Don't let her arrive at grade-school age and then let her go. You're not finished yet.

Don't let her get to her teenage years and then let her go. You're not finished yet.

Don't let yourself think, *Well, I've done pretty well so far. She has her driver's license and is pretty independent. After all, I did make it all the way to New Jersey.*

Building this girl is your job, it's going to take longer than you think, and you've got to make it the whole way to the end. And because you have determined not to take the easy way out by letting someone else finish what you started, you will be setting a high standard in your home.

"That's my dad. That's my husband. Take a look at how he does things with all his heart. He's not easily distracted from what he sets his mind to do. And notice . . . he's a 'finisher.'"

This will be music.

A Free Agent

Having said all this about not quitting, I need to remind you of what you're learning already. Your girl is a free agent. Nothing you can do will ever force her into a certain kind of thinking or behavior. Like it or not, there are no guarantees. There are no risk-free formulas. You're dealing with a person who has her own agenda, her own mind, and her own will. Ultimately, she'll think and do what she decides to think and do.

However, and this is a big *however*, you *can* create an environment that gives you—and her—the best shot at success. There are

> *You're dealing with a person who has her own agenda, her own mind, and her own will.*

certain things you can do that will raise your probability of success.

That's what this book is about—low-risk fathering.

STEP RIGHT UP

I've never been a successful gambler. Who knows, maybe if I had experienced some success early in life, I would have wound up in a Las Vegas gutter, homeless and broke. The few times I tried my hand at gambling—or even simple betting—I got burned in a major way.

As a kid, I could single-handedly break my favorite Major League Baseball team's winning streak by betting they'd win one more game. If you're also a Cubs fan, I'm sorry to have been the sole reason for their perennial failure.

In college, I participated in a chain-letter kind of get-rich-quick scheme using United States Savings Bonds. Since I was introduced to it by a CPA, the father of a good friend in Chicago, I figured it was kosher. So I brought it to campus and got it started.

A forerunner to things going viral on the Internet, this letter encouraged recipients to make copies and pass them around to friends who would also make copies and pass them around to their friends. In this case, the letter promised overnight riches if you got enough people to participate.

Just as it was really getting off the ground, Sam Delcamp, our dean of students, called me into his office and told me to shut it down or I'd be expelled from school. I thought about arguing with him about this draconian sentence, but the look on his face clearly informed me that there was no room for negotiation. That night and the next few nights, I went door to door in every men's dormitory on campus, requesting that the chain letter be stopped. I also asked each man how much money he would personally lose by stopping the letter immediately. I wrote the information down and promised to pay the money back to every one of them, which cost me all my wages from the next summer's construction work.

For some reason, regular, garden-variety gambling has been very, very bad to me.

I know that this may sound cold, arbitrary, and unspiritual, but fathering your daughter well is a gamble. It's about odds-making and long shots. It's about rolling the dice and holding your breath. It's about doing your best and then hoping, believing, and praying—especially praying.

In his best-selling book *Parenting Isn't for Cowards*, Dr. James Dobson talks to parents who, despite doing everything right, have children who turn out wrong. Naturally they feel guilty about it.

For illustration, he tells the story of a bunch of balloons.

He and his wife, Shirley, were attending an outdoor wedding where, the moment the bridegroom kissed his new bride, many brilliantly colored, helium-filled balloons were released.[1]

At first the balloons seemed to hang together. But soon the slight breeze began to separate them . . . some by large spaces.

Most of those brightly colored delights soared higher and higher. A few, however, seemed to have difficulty. Instead of sailing upward, they hovered near the treetops. Some even brushed along high-tension electrical wires, exploding with a loud pop.

Isn't it interesting that all those balloons, filled with the same kind of helium and released at the same moment, could have such diverse ends?

Dr. Dobson's point was meant as an encouragement to parents whose children were the hovering kind rather than the soaring kind—especially those parents with more than one child, all of whom had received similar input but with different results. The same parents, with basically the same external influences, experienced greatly diverse outcomes.

So did this story mean you should just spontaneously throw yourself at this job of building your daughter with no plan, hoping for the best, believing that what will be, will be?

No, absolutely not!

SAFETY FIRST

I used to think football players lifted weights and ran wind sprints so they could win. But actually, winning is the second most important reason they endure all that training pain.

During the early spring of 1994, I had the opportunity to walk through the new North Dallas training facility of the Cowboys with safety Bill Bates. Bill had the reputation of being one of the toughest men ever to play professional football. His specialty—special teams—was putting his head down and crashing into ball carriers, headfirst,[2] punishing them for catching the punt or kickoff. It was great fun watching number 40 play. In fact, I remember hoping the Cowboys would go three and out so I could watch Bill do his special-team thing. John Madden put him on the All-Madden team every year. In fact, in his book *Hey, Wait a Minute*, Madden identified Bill Bates and Reggie White as his "heroes."[3]

So as Bill and I were walking through this sparkling new facility, I asked him about working out and why he did it four to six hours per day year-round.

I was surprised to hear his answer. The primary reason he endured the pain of daily workouts was to *protect* himself from being seriously hurt on the field. Bill explained that if the other men on the field were in better condition than he was, his chances for serious injury were exponentially greater. The only reason more players aren't literally killed in action is that they're in great shape. How else could they walk away from some of those incredible collisions?

They build their muscles to lower—although, unfortunately, not to eliminate—the risk of serious injury. It's gambling with the odds in their favor.

When I use one of my power tools, I always wear goggles. Why? Well, in addition to making me look cool to the neighbors ("Wow, Robert must be doing something dangerous. See, he's wearing protective eyewear!"), they lower the risk of eye injury. Do they totally eliminate the risk? No. I suppose that even though they're made with space-age plastic, something *could* fly up and shatter them in my face. I wear them because working with power equipment is a gamble. The spinning blade or twirling bit will happily shoot something toward my face and take out an eye. My bet is that I won't get hurt. The goggles improve my chances of being right.

You're a dad. You have a daughter, and raising her to be a happy and well-balanced woman is not an absolute certainty. It's a gamble.

Because of what the Bible describes as a "sinful nature," her tug will probably be toward jumping off the track on her journey toward completeness. The magnetic draw of her culture will tempt her away from what's clean and pure and right. Her friends may whisper to her that her parents are empty-headed prudes—icons from a former century. Without any help from you, she will lean toward selfishness and a lack of discipline. And disobedience.

Your hope, your every effort—your bet—is that she's going to stay on a good track. You are the eyewear that stands in the way of those things that could injure her—the shard of pretty broken glass that she finds on the street . . . or the paralyzing emotions that whisper to her uncertain and developing mind that her daddy doesn't really love her or that she's not a precious child of God.

Doing what this book suggests won't guarantee that your protection will prevail. However, I promise that doing what it suggests will increase your odds of success.

So consider the next seven chapters to be free weights and treadmills; laps around the track and stair machines; fathering goggles.

My hope is that you'll not only make it through but will also enjoy *victory*—the safe completion of a daughter . . . and that beautiful wooden deck and lots of juicy burgers or sizzling salmon on that gas grill.

And don't forget to finish. Go all the way to the very end.

You can do it.

Builder's Checklist

1. It's a lot easier to start projects than it is to finish them. But when you do push ahead, resisting the temptation to quit, you discover a payoff that's well worth the sacrifice.

2. Now that your daughter is home, she's a keeper. You can't take her back for a refund.

3. Professional football players get in shape to reduce their odds of injury. Doing the right thing with your daughter won't guarantee success, but it will increase your chances.

4. Someone has joked that he finds himself praying, "Lord, give me patience . . . and give it to me now!" Of course, praying for patience is no laughing matter. Take some time—right now seems like a good opportunity—and pray for patience with your daughter. If you need help, pray the following:

Lord, I am a quitter. It's much easier for me to start than to finish. And there are times when I get very impatient with _____ . *Sometimes I feel like a failure, and I want to quit. Lord, I confess that I need You to help me persevere. Please help me be a loving, gracious, enduring, and patient dad. Oh, and thank You so much for my daughter. Amen.*

PART TWO

Never Too Tough, Never Too Tender— Seven Things You Must Know

PROTECTION

Able to Leap Tall Buildings in a Single Bound

> *It is difficult to give children a sense of*
> *security unless you have it yourself. If*
> *you have it, they catch it from you.*
> —Dr. William C. Menninger

I made the decision to do something about dating way back when our second daughter, Julie, was in sixth grade. She had, unbeknownst to us, agreed to "go with" another sixth-grader named Vincent. Two months after this "romance" had begun, Vincent called our house. Missy, Julie's older sister, answered the phone. After identifying himself, Vincent asked Missy if Julie was home. She wasn't. So Vincent asked Missy to give Julie the following message: "Tell her she's dumped."

I decided we could do better than this.

Four years later, Julie turned 16. One evening as I wheeled my car into our driveway after work, a shiny, two-door European sedan parked in front of our house caught my eye. "Nice," I remember whispering out loud. "Very nice."

Steven was a senior. I had already suspected he was interested in Julie because of his recent visits to our church and Sunday school. The kid was a Roman Catholic, but suddenly he was interested in becoming a Presbyterian.

Julie was only a week short of her 16th birthday, and Steven knew the rules: No one-on-one dating until Julie had turned 16; and boys had to be interviewed. By me.

After parking my car in the garage, I walked through the kitchen into the family room, where Bobbie, Julie, and Steven were sitting, making small talk.

Steven quickly stood. "Good evening, Mr. Wolgemuth," he said, squeezing out a thin, nervous smile.

"Hi, Steven. How are you?" I replied, firmly shaking his hand.

"Fine." His lips were white.

Following a few seconds of silence, I spoke again. "How about if we go into the next room for a few minutes?"

His visit to our house was to get this meeting out of the way. He knew it was part of the deal, and he was ready.

Steven was tall and handsome, with steel-blue eyes, curly blond hair, very straight teeth, and a winsome smile. He was a varsity basketball player with a physique to match. He followed me into my study, where I invited him to sit in the chair across from my desk.

Again, after just a moment of silence, I broke in. "I couldn't help but notice the car out front when I drove in," I said. "Is it yours?"

"Yes, sir," Steven replied, displaying his best Southern manners. "My dad is helping with the payments, but I cover the insurance and gas. We bought it last summer, and I've spent a lot of time fixing it up. The engine was in pretty good shape, but the body needed some work, especially the rear quarter panels on both sides."

This was a lot more information than I was looking for, but I let him run. He was taking the bait. After listening to a few more minutes of detail about what he had done to the car, I leaned back in my chair and smiled.

"It sounds like this is a pretty special car," I said, leading him deeper. He nodded as I continued: "Now, can I ask you a question?"

"Okay, go ahead," he replied.

"What if I had come to your house last night, knocked on the door, and asked if I could borrow your car for the evening? What would you have said?"

Steven took no time to respond: "I'd have said, 'No way.'"

Poor kid, I thought. *You've had it now.* I waited for just a few moments. A little drama wasn't going to hurt.

"Why?" I replied, acting as though his answer fascinated me.

"Well, because I don't know you. I don't know how you drive. I don't know how you'd treat my car. I'm not sure I can trust you. That car's important to me." Steven's narrowed eyes let me know he was very serious.

When he finished, I leaned forward on my elbows, taking just a moment to make sure he was listening carefully. "That's interesting, Steven," I finally said. "I know exactly what you're saying. If I were you, I'd do the same thing."

He smiled and, for the first time, looked a little relaxed. Some color was returning to his lips. "You would?" he said.

"Absolutely," I reassured him. "And do you want to know why?" I gave him no time to answer. "Because tonight you've come to my house and asked if you can come back next weekend to *borrow* our daughter for the evening. And before I let you do that, I want to find out who you are."

A shocked but dawning look of understanding crossed his face— an interesting mix of discovery and nausea. I had his undivided attention. I double-checked to be sure he was breathing. He was.

Believe it or not, the conversation that followed wasn't adversarial. I actually found myself liking Steven. He seemed like a nice young man. As we talked, I reminded him that, as an 18-year-old, he was far more experienced than Julie. I expected him to treat her the way he treated his four-wheeled import. No, actually, better.

He understood.

We talked about what was important to him—his sports, his family, his favorite subjects in school, his plans for next year, and his faith. I told him a little about our family and assured him he would always be welcome in our home. I told him our daughter's friends were our friends. He seemed appreciative.

When we finished our conversation, we both stood up. I reached out and shook his hand. He looked at me as though he had something to say. I paused, smiled, and nodded toward him, making it easier for him to speak.

"You know, Mr. Wolgemuth," he said, "if I ever have a 16-year-old daughter of my own, I'll do what you did today."

"Thank you, Steven," I replied. "It means a lot that you would say that."

I walked him to the family room, where Bobbie and Julie were waiting. They later told me they had been praying for him.

"Good-bye, Steven," I said. "I'll see you around."

"Good-bye, Mr. Wolgemuth."

Julie walked Steven to the front door and said good-bye. I watched him hustle to his waiting car. He seemed eager to get going.

In a few days, Steven would be back to pick Julie up for her first date. He'd be back in his shiny car to take our daughter. Out.

PROTECTION FROM . . .

In one of our scrapbooks is a picture that Bobbie took of me in 1971, lying on my stomach across our bed. I'm sleeping, and my arms are next to me in a curved position, like the right-turn signal you learned in bicycle safety. Sleeping inside the space made by my arm and my head is this miniature person. Missy's head is no bigger than my palm. Her little clenched hands are the size of walnuts.

In the photo, she looks so fragile and absolutely breakable. And she was.

Your job as a dad is to protect your daughter. Of course, the nature of your protection changes as your daughter grows, and it's your job to make the adjustments appropriately. When she's crawling toward a roaring fireplace, you yank her back. When her little bicycle is heading for the street, you sprint down the driveway to stop it. When you introduce her to an electronic device that has high-speed Internet access from anywhere, you pay careful attention. And when you launch her into the hostile environment of growing up, you stand guard.

> *The nature of your protection changes as your daughter grows.*

Why? Because she needs it. And, as we'll talk about later, she wants it.

The need for protection is evident when your girl is small. Nearly everything presents its own unique opportunity for potential danger.

"Be careful of the stove, honey, the kettle is hot. Hot. Haaahhhttt!" You act as if you're touching the kettle yourself. You quickly pull your hand back. Your eyes get big. "Ooowwwweeee. See, sweetheart? Hot."

"Leave that doggie alone, baby. Look at those big teeth! I think he's angry. He might bite you if you don't stop pulling his ear. Let's see if we can find something else to do."

"No, sweetie," you say. "Your iPad isn't able to search the net without my supervision. Daddy put some special software on it."

Your job is to provide a safe haven. Whether it's keeping your daughter from being attacked by a coiled snake lurking in your vegetable garden or from the longing eyes of an 18-year-old athlete, or the waiting photo images online, your job is to protect. And you're the one man in her life who has from the beginning had nothing but the purest intentions for her.

I've Got Everything
Under Control . . . Almost

I learned an important lesson the hard way about the need to keep an eye on small children. On an award-winning, springtime Saturday morning when we lived in Geneva, Illinois, Bobbie told me she was going to spend several hours with a friend at a craft bazaar. My job was to watch the girls, who were four and a half and one and a half at the time.

I assured her I would have everything under control. *How hard can it be to babysit the girls for a few hours?*

Over the years, I've discovered that many dads think of an assignment like "Keep an eye on the kids" the same way they would regard a request to "Keep an eye on the smoke alarm fastened to their kitchen ceiling." If it's not wailing at plaster-cracking decibels, it must be okay.

That Saturday morning, I was one of those dads.

I was sitting cross-legged on the garage floor, sharpening the blade on my lawn mower with a large file. Since it was like staring into an alligator's open mouth, I had made sure the gas tank was empty, propping the mower back so I could easily reach the blade. The garage door was open and the girls were in the front yard, playing Duck Duck Goose with their friend Laura Green. Except for an occasional happy squeal, I heard nothing. All seemed well.

After a while, Missy came into the garage to retrieve the stroller. Their game had lost its charm, and she and Laura were going to take Julie for a little ride. "Be careful," I warned in a dad-like voice with an I-really-care vocal lift at the end. I didn't even look up. *Girls are so easy*, I thought.

Our stroller was an inexpensive and flimsy portable model that folded into something not much bigger than an umbrella. (This was before the government set standards that now require strollers to be substantial enough to transport a bass boat.) For the next several minutes, Missy and Laura took turns pushing Julie back and forth on the sidewalk in front of our house.

Then, because young girls can get bored quickly, they decided to make up a new game. This game was called "Let's take the stroller to the top of our steep driveway and see how fast we can get it going on its own"—with Julie still on board, of course.

Oblivious to the girls' new game, I continued to file away. My lawn mower blade was looking good. *This thing will take out small trees,* I proudly mused.

Missy stood at the top of the driveway. Laura waited at the bottom to keep Julie and the stroller from flying into the street. They were all having a big time. But apparently, after a few breakneck voyages to the sidewalk, Julie decided to get creative. *I wonder what would happen if I took my feet off this little footrest and tried to stop this thing myself,* she must have thought, because the next time down, she jammed her little sneakers down onto the asphalt.

The physics of the speeding stroller wouldn't allow for tiny, screeching shoes to bring it to a safe stop. Instead, the stroller flipped forward, end over end, until it came to rest at the bottom of the driveway.

The smoke alarm began to wail—no, actually, two alarms . . . Missy and Laura Green.

By the time I reached the scene of the accident, Missy was out of control. Laura had already run home and was making plane reservations for Paraguay.

Julie, still partially in the stroller, was silently lying on her side, her nose and lips bleeding. Sheer panic swept over me. *How long does it take for this kind of thing to heal? I wonder if she'll be okay by the time Bobbie gets back?*

Julie was not crying. The impact had almost knocked her unconscious. I knelt down and talked to her. Her eyes opened slowly. I tried reassuring her that she was all right . . . which, of course, I was hoping. Suddenly I thought, *I wonder what this did to her teeth?*

Gently opening her mouth, I was met with a horrible sight. The full force of the initial impact must have centered on Julie's face, slamming her mouth into the driveway. The black tar from the asphalt had left scrape marks on her front teeth. With all the blood from her lips, I had no idea if they were chipped or, worse, broken off.

I'm a dead man, raced through my mind. *How will I ever explain this to Bobbie?*

The truth is, I had failed. My job had been to watch the girls, and I hadn't.

When Bobbie got home, she let me have it. I asked if she wanted to see how sharp my lawn mower blade was. She didn't.

Gratefully, Julie's baby teeth were only slightly chipped, and the swollen lips healed nicely. But that spring day, I learned a vital lesson: Protecting my daughters can never be a careless afterthought.

And these protections will change as she grows; the problems with leaving her unsupervised will look different. The need for your attention is not always evident, but the danger is no less real. It won't be a chipped tooth; it'll be a chipped heart. And she will need you.

PHYSICAL PROTECTION

If there's one word to describe your baby when you bring her home from the hospital, it's *helpless*. This baby can do absolutely nothing for herself. She would literally perish without constant care. Her needs are for physical protection.

From that moment on, however, her physical helplessness will diminish a day at a time. Each new step in her development will announce one more place where she can do things herself. From holding her head up on the changing table and tying her own shoes all the way to finding her way through big-city traffic driving *your* car, she'll need your physical protection less and less.

Many years ago, Dr. Jay Kesler told a story about the protective habits of one Mother Wren. The wren family is perched high in a tree enjoying their lovely, one-story nest. Mother Wren conceives, lays four little eggs, and patiently keeps them warm until they hatch. Daddy Wren passes out cigars to every man bird in the neighborhood, including the crow who loves to smoke. What other explanation would there be for that coarse voice?

As her chicks' fuzzy down begins turning into real feathers, the mother decides it's time for flying lessons. Because this wise parent understands the value of diminishing physical protection, she takes her babies on a short journey, a hopping field trip just a few feet down the branch and then safely back to the nest.

Several days later, the journey takes the awkward little birds a bit farther down the branch—but always under the mother's watchful eye.

Eventually Mother Wren, determining that her brood is ready to challenge the neighborhood cat, kicks them out of the nest to fly on their own. Interestingly, the wrens with their newfound freedom still return to the nest for several days. Soon, however, they're gone forever to live in a sorority house with dozens of other birds. Daddy Wren works overtime hours because he has agreed to pay the school tuition.

This is exactly as it should be—progressive physical independence. Your daughter is taught, she experiences growth and development, and then she actually exercises those new, independent characteristics and skills.

CHILDPROOFING AND MONITORING

When your daughter begins to crawl, you're going to have to childproof your house. Anything she can crawl to and open, break, or pull down on herself has to be removed.

When Missy and Julie were this age, we put safety catches on all the kitchen and bathroom cabinet doors. What a nuisance they were!

But dishwashing detergent and toilet-bowl cleaner look mighty delicious when you're six months old.

Tall, thin end tables or plant stands are easily pulled down as your little girl learns the art of pulling herself up from her knees. And delicate glass figurines or sharp objects need to be moved to a high shelf. Don't worry, you'll be able to restore everything to its rightful place before you know it. Oh, you're going to have lots more kids? Maybe you ought to go ahead and have a garage sale or give some of this stuff away as gifts. (Isn't that where *you* got them?)

The dog's water and the cat's litter box are going to have to go somewhere too. Don't ask me where; we didn't have pets until the girls were much older. We *tried* a puppy when Missy was a couple of years old, but she kept putting its face in her mouth. So long, puppy.

After those first steps, the plot thickens. In no time, you're going to wonder why you were so eager to see your little girl walk! The crawling trip from the living room to the kitchen, which used to take a few minutes, now seems almost instantaneous. Before you can send a three-word text message to your colleague, you look up and she's gone.

Keep an eye on her.

PROTECTING HER ELECTRONICALLY

At the risk of sounding like a pterodactyl, I never saw my young daughters with anything in their hands that had an illuminated screen. Yes, we did have a black-and-white television, but it was way too big for a child to pick up. And we only had three—count them, one, two, three—choices for viewing. If it wasn't on NBC, CBS, or ABC, it wasn't on.

Then in 1980, the year that Missy turned nine and Julie turned six, CNN—and 24/7 news—was born. That made four choices. Today that number is close to 2,000 broadcast channels.

In 1971 and 1974, when our girls were born, no one other than the military had heard of the Internet. Civilians would have been hard-pressed even to dream of such a thing.

The term *website* meant only that a spider had made his home somewhere in the corner. Now, if you wanted to take the time, you could count about three quarters of a billion websites in the world—unique "channels"—where information or entertainment can be found. And these are easily accessed by everyone . . . including your daughter.[1]

Please let me quickly say that I'm not standing on a street corner, shouting through a bullhorn. I am not denouncing all this high-speed stuff. I'm actually very thankful for much of it. It has made my life and yours a lot easier. Professionally, these gadgets have helped me build my small business with multiple virtual offices into a category leader. Relationally, being able to shoot a text message to someone I love is a remarkable joy.

But what I am saying is that, with the advent of the little handheld screen and keypad, the world of parenting has changed. Completely.

Getting her undivided attention when she has an illuminated screen in front of her is not possible, mostly because you and I are not as interesting. If you are speaking to her and she's tapping on a screen, she is not listening.

The other sobering reality of your daughter's fascination with electronics is that she's literally holding in her hand a portal of incoming information that gives predators unrestricted access.

Maybe this illustration will help.

Does your daughter's bedroom have a lock? Do you need a key to open the door?

Well, the door may have a privacy lock, with a little hole in the center of the knob, that makes entry impossible without one of those metal pins you keep handy on the molding above the door frame for emergencies—like when your 18-month-old permanently secures herself in the bathroom and cannot get out.

But for your daughter's bedroom, there's probably no lock that needs a key to open it. Right? However, let's pretend that your daughter's bedroom *does* have such a lock.

If you let your daughter walk into her bedroom with her cell phone or iPad in hand, close the door, and lock it, you have just handed her bedroom key to millions of people—primarily men—some who would be pleased to harm her. She also can see millions of harmful images with a simple tap or two on the screen. Your daughter's cell phone or iPad or laptop grants complete strangers a key to freely access her room—and her mind. Also, when she logs on to a site, the owner of that site can sometimes acquire her name and address.

This is a chapter about protection. The first—and maybe most important—thing you need to do to protect your daughter from those thousands of people who could hurt her is to tell them all to turn in their keys to the nice man at the front desk. If anyone has a key to her room, it will be you . . . and your wife.

No one else.

THE PROCESS OF PHYSICALLY UNPROTECTING

While your daughter is still in your nest, hands-on protection for her comes in the form of physically taking your child away from danger. Your girl depends on you to make all her protective decisions. If she's close to danger, you yank her away from it. No discussion. No questions asked.

Soon, you demonstrate and teach about danger. Eventually, that gives way to allowing her to test what she's learned. You let her dance a few feet away from the nest and then back again—nothing involving life and death.

After years of watchful protection, you don't suddenly say to your child, "Well, I've been protecting you from all these dangerous things, but now it's time you learned how to fend for yourself. So your mother and I are going away for the weekend. Before we leave, we'll turn on all the computers and log on to the network, put all the cleansers and prescription drugs out where you can get to them, and then just set you loose in here. When we get back, if you've survived, we'll set your toy box on the street, where you can spend the next day."

No, as she grows, you "invite" her out of the nest a few feet at a time. You give her a chance to spread her wings just a little—a chance where, if she makes a mistake, she hasn't done any severe damage to herself or anyone else.

Yes, you may go ahead and buy her a smartphone or iPod when she's very young, but you put limits on its use. And you don't succumb to the pressure of wanting to be considered a cool dad. You set guidelines and you stick to them. You are not swayed by almost impenetrable forces like pleading, whining, or eye rolling. These things may be effective with some dads. But not you.

As your daughter grows, you, like the mother wren, let your chick hop out on the branch . . . go on some field trips away from you. The gradual move away from physically protecting your girl is a systematic process of showing and teaching her what's dangerous and what's safe.

THE BABYSITTING FIELD TRIP

Find money in your budget for babysitters. Of course, going out without your little one gives you and your wife some relief from the relentless demands of parenting. But leaving your girl with someone else also gives her a taste of independence—making decisions on her own regarding what's safe and what's not.

What she'll learn is that sharp things are sharp even if you and your wife are 10 miles away. Breakable things are still breakable even if you're not there to say your predictable "Be careful."

Occasionally Bobbie and I talk to parents who proudly announce that they haven't spent a night away from their two-year-old. Although I believe their motives—not wanting to expose their child to danger or the unpredictability of life without them—are admirable, they're forgetting the need to transition away from physical protection in a regular, systematic way, helping their child to make all of Mom's and Dad's verbal cautions their own through personal experience. *Hmm, Mom was right, jumping on the bed can lead to falling off the bed, and falling off the bed hurts. Wow, Dad was right, this knife* is *very sharp!*

FIELD TRIPS OUTSIDE THE HOME

Have you noticed there are couples who, after they have their first baby, seem to disappear from church? They were so faithful, and now they're gone. So you call them and discover they're afraid the little one will be exposed to physical danger or germs. "We're going to keep the baby home for a few years," they say.

> *If God didn't think He could protect your baby in His own house, why would He have created nurseries?*

This is faulty thinking, because if God didn't think He could protect your baby in His own house, why would He have created nurseries?

Church is going to be a hop down the branch for your girl. She's going to learn that your admonition to "Be nice to other children" is for her own protection. You'll be sitting there in "big church," singing your favorite worship song, and your daughter will either witness or personally experience—you hope it's witness—the pain of retaliation for the unauthorized "borrowing" of another child's toy. And she'll think, *Hmm, Daddy was right. Sharing doesn't hurt as much as not sharing does!*

A successful field trip.

Grade school is another example of where other children come into play. Fellow students will usually provide solid companionship for your daughter, and rarely do they present physical dangers. However, the need for your emotional protection begins to climb at this stage. If you're particularly concerned about this, perhaps a martial arts course for your daughter at your neighborhood YMCA would be a good idea. Or you could homeschool.

EMOTIONAL PROTECTION

Your daughter's need for your emotional protection is far less visible or predictable than her need for physical protection. Its form may change from day to day, but it's just as important. Physical protection may seem more urgent when your girl is a tiny baby. But as she grows and relates more and more with others, the need for your emotional protection also grows.

Soon after we brought our first girl home from the hospital, I developed an interest in gardening. No one was more surprised than I was, since yard work had been nothing but drudgery from the time I had been able to push an unmotorized lawn mower. But my older brother, Ken, had introduced me to roses, and I remembered how beautiful they were. So I bought a couple dozen prizewinners and was off and running.

One particular June weekend, I was behind the house, clipping, dusting, pruning, fertilizing, and spraying my roses. Out of the corner of my eye, I noticed Missy, three and a half then, dashing through the yard toward the back door. She opened it just wide enough for her face and called, "Mommy!"

"Yes, Missy," came the voice of her mother from the other end of the house.

"Are you there?"

"Of course, Missy," came the reply. "I'm here."

Closing the door without stepping into the house, Missy ran around to the front again.

I continued to work on my roses, curious about what I had seen.

Several minutes later, Missy appeared again, running to the back door. Once more she opened it just enough for her little face and called out, "Mommy!"

"Yes, Missy, what is it?"

"Are you there?"

"Yes, honey, I'm here."

Again she closed the door and returned to the front of the house. Curiosity got the best of me, so I crept around to the front of the house to see what was going on.

Two of the older neighborhood girls had drawn a hopscotch court on the sidewalk with a piece of chalk. After playing several games alone, they apparently had invited Missy to join in. However, at three and a half, she hadn't been briefed on how to play the game. Instead of teaching her what to do, the older girls had left Missy to figure it out for herself. And, of course, she was doing it wrong—wrong square, wrong leg, wrong everything. This provided the older girls a little comic relief at Missy's expense.

In her little spirit, she knew something was wrong. So once Missy had finished her turn, she laid her little stone on the sidewalk and ran around to the back door. Somehow understanding that she was being laughed at, she needed the emotional protection of her mother's voice. And, apparently, it was enough. She returned to hopscotch on the front sidewalk and was ready for her next turn.

PROTECT, DON'T LECTURE

Dads are especially susceptible to turning an emotion-protecting opportunity into a veritable classroom, good enough for credit at the local junior college.

Bobbie and I have friends, Dave and Jan, whose daughter, Ashley, came running through the family room door one time when she was five years old. She was sobbing between deep gasps. When they had finally calmed her down enough for her to speak, she told them about the little girl across the street—how she had grabbed Ashley's finger painting from school (one more crinkly and brittle underwater seascape, soon to be displayed on the refrigerator door) and torn it in half.

"My first impulse," Dave later told me, "was to ask a few questions. Seize the moment. 'Why did your friend do such an ugly thing to you? What did *you* do to make her so unhappy? You *must* have done something to upset her.' Then I realized that my little girl did not need a lecture. This was not a teaching opportunity for me."

Dave put his reading down. He turned to his daughter and opened his arms. He held her until the crying had subsided. He didn't say a thing.

"What dawned on me, as my daughter's tears began soaking through my shirt," Dave told me, "was that life was about angry neighborhood kids. About injustice. And about consequences. Ashley was crying, and whatever had happened, she was paying for it with her own tears. She needed safety. Protection. So I gave it to her. A lecture—brilliant as it might have been—would have ruined this tender moment. The lesson had already been learned. There would be other times for lectures."

Whose Garden Is This?

In 1971, our company moved into a new office building. It was out in an area that someday would be completely developed with commercial buildings, but ours was the first building on a new street. Since there was a lot of open space around us, we asked the developer if we could parcel out some land among our employees for vegetable gardens.

He said that would be no problem. He warned us, however, that if the land should sell before harvest time, we'd have to understand. Tomato plants don't hold up well when confronted by a bulldozer's scoop.

So I became a gentleman farmer. It was great. I rented a rototiller, got the dirt all nice and loose, and bought seeds. (If you ever do this, buy squash. Zucchini will make you feel powerful as a gardener. Those huge leaves grow almost overnight.) Having my very own vegetable garden was so much fun.

Because this garden was a few hundred yards from any water sources, I had to water it by hand. And as it got into late June and early July, my plants didn't look as good as they had before. So one day I went out and had a little talk with my garden. I said to those plants, "You're a disgrace. Just look at you. I mean, you're getting all ugly and brown. Some of your lower leaves are falling off. Some of them are wilted. Some of them even look dead. You ought to be ashamed."

To be honest, that conversation didn't really happen. Actually, June was a little dry that year, and those leaves *did* get a little brown. But I decided that if I was going to enjoy any harvest, I would have to carry water. I let them die instead. That's why there's a produce department at our grocery store.

Sometimes a foolish dad surveys his family and says, "Just look at you. You're misbehaved and out of control. You never look at me when I'm talking to you. That stupid cell phone (or whatever) is apparently more important than me. And you grumble all the time about the things your friends have that are better than yours. Come on, kids, shape up."

Guess whose responsibility this protection and nurture thing is? Guess who's responsible, even on a hot July day after you've put in a full day of your own work, to "carry the water," even if you have to carry it in jugs a few hundred yards? With a daughter, you don't have the option to stop nurturing.

Yes, it's a lot of work. But you *can* do this.

"How Did It Make You Feel When . . . ?"

There's a magic phrase that will unlock your girl's emotions and give you an opportunity to protect her. I encourage you, even when she's just beginning to talk, to start lots of questions with it: "How did it make you feel when . . . ?"

After my friend Dave had held Ashley long enough for her tears to subside, his first question to her should have been, "How did it make you feel when the little girl tore your paper in half?" And, as Ashley was describing what hurt feelings looked like to her, Dave should have been listening carefully, occasionally saying things like "I understand" and "That must really make you sad."

In doing this, Dave would have been giving Ashley permission to express her emotional pain. He would also have been giving her a safe environment—a protected place—in which to express it. Sometimes genuine sympathy is more important than answers, a fact that can be especially difficult for a man who's hopelessly addicted to fixing everything.

Professionals tell us that when emotional pain is locked in the subconscious mind, it often gets infected, creating a far more dangerous situation in later years. Your invitation to your girl to tell you how she's feeling will bring those emotions into the light of day, giving them a chance to be thoroughly expressed . . . and to heal.

BOYS . . . A REPRISE

When each of our girls turned 13, I took them out to dinner. I chose a place they would consider special. What was important was that *they* thought it was a big deal.

During the dinner, I explained to them that over the next few years, there would be other men in their lives. Young men would begin to notice them and, perhaps, like them and want to date them.

Then I presented my daughters with a gift. Missy got a key with a tiny diamond chip on the top, and Julie got a ring. I called Missy's gift the "key to her heart" and Julie's her "promise ring." But they both meant the same thing: Until I walked them down the aisle and gave them away to a man other than me, I held the key to their hearts. Their purity was something to be treasured and worth protecting.

When the time was right, the key or the ring would be given to someone else who would love and cherish them—difficult as it is to believe—as much as their dad did. Neither of them forgot that moment.

The story of my interviewing Steven is an example of fairly thorough emotional protection. I was exercising my right to keep Julie from being hurt by this older boy. And although I wasn't angry and avoided making any specific threats, I was putting him on notice: Be careful with this girl. She belongs to a family that cares for her.

When our daughters were out of the house and on their own, was I still protecting them from boys? No. Why? Because I wasn't around. They were hours from me. But when they were 16 years old, my job was to show them *how* to interview a boy while experiencing the security of my protection. Then I helped them learn how to conduct an "interview" themselves—how to ask boys good questions on their own. (See the next chapter on conversation.) Believe it or not, a college or career young woman can have just as much power in an interview with a potential suitor as her dad did when she was 16. Just ask a couple of college or career men.

When my friends heard that I was interviewing Julie's potential dates, I remember some of them asking me how Julie put up with it. "Man, if I tried that with my daughter's dates, she'd kill me," they said.

I understood this concern. The last thing a child wants or needs is a parent who takes protection to the extreme. When Missy and Julie were young, the term "helicopter parent" hadn't yet appeared in the lexicon of common expressions. But even the mother wren understood the difference between protecting and smothering.

So would these guys' daughters have resented their interviewing prospective boyfriends? No, probably not. The chances are strong that these daughters would have felt a sense of confidence and security. They would have the assurance that they weren't out in the open alone—that they were still protected in some way by the man who had protected them from the beginning.

They would also be assured that when there was a problem with something Dad was doing, they could talk to him about it. They could tell him the truth, and he would do his best to listen and not be defensive.

That's why the next chapter is so critical for you to read and understand.

Builder's Checklist

Protecting your girl is your job. It takes a lot of wisdom and patience. Here are a few reminders from this chapter:

1. *Be attentive to the protection seesaw.* As your daughter grows, her need for protection from physical dangers will diminish, but her need for protection from emotional danger will increase. When you're turning her away from the sharp objects and breakable figurines of life, turn her attention to something else. "Let's play with LEGOs" or "Let's go for a ride in Daddy's car" are a lot more effective than a stern *no.*

2. *Childproof your house.* Okay, so it's inconvenient to move everything fragile to an unreachable location, but do it anyway. If you don't, you'll be saying no during every one of your daughter's waking hours. Besides, she'll soon grow out of this, and your home decor will be restored in no time.

3. *Take her out . . . a lot.* Yes, there are germs out there. Yes, there are rowdy, block-hurling boys in the church nursery. Take her out anyway. Don't succumb to the temptation—or your wife's—to protect your daughter from this stuff. She'll be fine.

4. *Turn loose on time.* For some dads, turning their girl loose
    to hop down the branch is tough. When dads physically
    overprotect, their daughters develop an unhealthy, long-term
    dependence on them. Yes, buy her a phone or touch pad.
    (You'll be amazed at how quickly—instantly—she becomes
    adept at using it.) But do not be afraid to set limits. And stick
    to them. If you don't turn her loose little by little, your girl
    may not learn to make her own good decisions. She won't be
    able to renew a driver's license or fill out an insurance form.
    She'll be afraid to take a two-hour car trip on her own. Don't
    let this happen. Give your daughter a taste of physical inde-
    pendence when she's small. Sleepovers at a friend's house or a
    week of summer camp will help.

5. *Talk about feelings.* As you learn to protect your daughter's
    delicate emotions, also learn to ask about them. "How did
    that make you feel?" is a magic question. Always support her
    answer, too. You'll be tempted to argue with her feelings, but
    don't. If she's angry, let her be angry. Tell her, "If that had
    happened to me, I would probably be angry, too." If she's
    hurt, let her be hurt. Never say, "Oh, you don't—or you
    shouldn't—*really* feel that way." You'll shut her down, and
    she'll stop talking to you.

6. *Establish a babysitter fund.* No matter how small your salary,
    always set some money aside for babysitters. Your daughter
    will learn important independence lessons on someone else's
    watch. Hint: Find *girl* babysitters who come from families
    you know and trust, and whose dads have read this book. An-
    other hint: Just as soon as your girl is old enough, get her out
    there babysitting. It's a great way for her to earn a little extra
    money, but it's also a chance to learn while she's "teaching."
    She'll discover just how smart her dad really is.

7. *Interview her dates.* Although you'll have a lot of fun telling
    your friends about this one, it's not a laughing matter to your
    daughter. Don't let her overhear you bragging about how
    smart you are to be conducting the interview. This is an inti-
    mate thing between you and her. She's trusting you by letting
    you talk to her prospective boyfriends. Don't abuse that privi-
    lege. Remember, this interview is not about your approval of
    your daughter's choice in boys. Every boy passes your inspec-
    tion, regardless. (Gulp.) The very fact that the interview is
    going to take place will have a sorting effect all by itself. Our
    daughters told us that word about my interviews had spread
    around their school. Boys actually told them that they'd like
    to date them, but they wouldn't take part in an interview
    with their dad. Our daughters trusted me enough to be okay
    with that. No interview with my dad? No date. Done.

8. *Be as available as you can.* If you have an office job and you
    still use a landline phone, always let your daughter's call come
    through. Wherever you are, respond to her texts or phone
    calls quickly. This emotional protection thing is about good
    timing. And if you're not there when she needs it, she may get
    advice from someone else . . . possibly a younger man whose
    wisdom will be inferior to yours.

CONVERSATION

Just Keep Talking

*To talk to a child, to fascinate her, is much
more difficult than to win an electoral
victory. But it is also more rewarding.*
—SIDONIE-GABRIELLE COLETTE,
FRENCH AUTHOR

Taylor University, my college alma mater, had a dinnertime custom
for many years. Folklore had it that, over the years, many women had
transferred to other schools in order to get away from this tradition.

Every weekday evening, at exactly six o'clock, the doors of the dining hall would open, but only for the coeds. The ladies would stream
in, filling every other seat at the round, eight-person tables. They made
this processional to the strains of a classical piece on an ancient upright
piano in the corner, played, of course, by a music major.

Once the dining hall was exactly half filled, the men were released,
set free to prowl the tables, looking for a seat. In selecting where they
wanted to sit, they also chose where they *didn't* want to spend their
dinner hour. They'd look at an empty chair, then look at who'd they
be sitting next to if they selected that one. And then they'd look away
and move on. Now do you know why the women hated this practice?

Students waited tables, family-style. I'm sure a family atmosphere, with pleasant conversation, is just what the well-intentioned founders of the tradition had wanted to create.

Fortunately, in 1966, this tradition came to an end. The dean had reportedly succumbed to the subtle pressure of a mob of torch-carrying women.

I remember one dinner in the spring of my freshman year. I was sitting with seven classmates—three men and four women. We were engaged in the usual college chatter when someone mentioned the breakup of one of Taylor's "fixture" couples. He was a sophomore; she was a freshman—one of our own.

All the side conversations at the table stopped. Everyone wanted to hear about couples breaking up. It was like a live tabloid press conference. We weren't being hateful or nosey. No, just "fully informed."

One of the girls gave the report that it was Paula's decision to break off the relationship. "Irreconcilable differences," she said. Paula had loved Michael, but there was just no future in it.

"That's not what I heard," I glibly announced. "I heard that Michael really let her have it. He really hadn't liked her all that much from the beginning and just told her so. He broke her heart, but, oh well, these things happen." I was a veritable fountain of gossip that evening. I was holding court all by myself, and everyone was listening.

When I finished my thorough report, I took a breath and looked up into the faces of my classmates. They were ashen, gazing at me in disbelief. The boys in particular looked sick.

As I looked more closely, I discovered they weren't actually looking at me. They were looking just above me at—you guessed it—our family-style waitress.

I yanked around in my chair to see who had captured their attention. It was Paula.

Paula and I had been friends, often walking to classes together. As a friend, I liked Paula a lot. And until that moment when our eyes locked onto each other's for one very painful second, she had liked me.

I will remember that incident for the rest of my life—what it felt like to be sitting there, trapped in the cross fire of my friend's pain and the disbelieving stares of my seven tablemates. I don't recall ever feeling such embarrassment, such shame.

What I learned that instant was this truth: Words have unbelievable power. Clustered together well, they can restore and renew people. They can lift the heart and heal the spirit. They can build the character of the speaker and the esteem of the recipient. But, unfortunately, they also can cause great pain. And once spoken, they can never be unsaid.

The tongue has been accurately compared to the rudder of a ship (see James 3:4-5). With just a little instrument, an entire life can be set on the right course or perilously aimed at an iceberg.

THE CROWN JEWEL

Properly teaching the skills of conversation is the most critical thing a dad must do in building his little girl. The ability for you and your daughter to effectively exchange words—and the feelings they're usually connected to—will provide the bridge between you that will last the rest of your lives.

You'll quickly discover that, because she's a woman, your daughter is more than capable of making noise, even forming words at an early age. But she'll still need to learn how to talk. How to create dialogue. She won't pick this up properly without some help from you.

Actually, her very first word will likely be "dada." When she says that, you will be absolutely convinced

> *The ability of you and your daughter to effectively exchange words—and the feelings they're usually connected to—will provide the bridge between you that will last the rest of your lives.*

that she's responding to someone's question to her: "Who is the most incredible hunk of human virility on the face of the earth?" You'll be proud.

THE WORLD OF WORDS

From the time she's small, read books to your girl. By doing this, you'll introduce her to a world of imagination and truth. Read fun books, silly books, nursery rhymes, true-life adventures, and Bible storybooks. Your local library, bookstore, or Internet book supplier will provide you with all the help you need to find some good, old-fashioned ones with paper and printed words. Some smart digital books downloaded to your e-reader or tablet can include animated clips that will be great fun to watch together. Hold her on your lap as you do these things. Without ever having to lecture her, you'll be showing your daughter how wonderful words can be.

From the time she's small, you must also teach your girl to honor conversation—words connecting two human beings. This lesson usually comes in the form of her attempts to interrupt you when you're talking to your wife or another adult.

The first time—and every time—this happens, you must stop talking—midsentence, if necessary. Then you look at your girl and you make sure that she's looking at you. You say, "Honey, I was talking with your mother. Please don't interrupt us when we're talking. Just as soon as we're finished, you and I can talk. I promise. Do you understand?"

Then, when you and your wife are done, go to your daughter and ask what she has to say. She may have forgotten, and that's okay. Don't shame her with "Hey, if you're going to interrupt me, you'd better have something important to say."

Instead, take a few minutes and have a conversation. And whatever you do, protect this little talk from any interruptions, even one that comes from an adult. As you're talking to your girl, also make sure your eyes connect. Don't glance at your phone or let your mind wander, either. Hang in there as long as you possibly can.

By listening carefully while she's speaking, you will be telling her nonverbally that conversation is very important. You'll also be communicating your love for her.

How Many Cows Can You Count over There?

When your girl is small, there really aren't that many interesting things you can talk about. You live in a world that's foreign to her. You've got pressure at work and are struggling to pay all your bills. She's got a broken toy teacup or a dolly who scraped her knee. So you'll have to find some things to discuss and places to discuss them.

No problem.

A good friend taught me a fathering lesson early in my parenting.

"On the weekends, never go anywhere alone," he told me. Simple advice with wonderful consequences. Taking his counsel, I rarely went out for errands on the weekend alone. I took Missy or Julie along—usually one at a time so we'd have each other's full attention.

As we were driving, I would ask questions. "Look over there in that field. Have you ever seen so many cows? I wonder how many there are." My daughter would look and start counting.

Or we'd play games. "Between here and the store," I'd say, "let's count how many trucks we pass." Or, "If you were an animal in the zoo, what animal would you like to be?"

If you follow my recommendation to take your daughter along on weekend errands, I encourage you—double-dog dare you—to leave your cell phone on vibrate and look at it only if you get an important message from your wife, like "An asteroid just landed on our house" or "You're a hunk" or "Can you stop and pick up some milk and eggs on your way home?" And if your daughter is old enough—at least six months—to have her own phone, she can leave it behind. For you and for her, these things can be mortal enemies of good conversation.

Early in our lives together, we built a connection of words, a bridge between a little girl and her daddy that inextricably bound us together.

The Gift That Keeps on Giving

Several years ago, our company posted a classified ad to help fill an open position. After I spent a full and exhausting day meeting prospective employees, one thing was clear: Some of those people had been taught how to carry on a conversation, and some hadn't. Those who knew the art had a shot at the job. Those who didn't, didn't.

Teaching your girl how to talk is like giving her a wonderful gift, one she'll enjoy for the rest of her life. In describing good conversation, James Dobson uses the helpful illustration of playing catch with a tennis ball. When you want to speak to someone, you "throw" the person a question. When he or she answers, the person is throwing a response back. Once you've caught the response, you toss another question.

Several years ago, we had a houseguest who stayed with us for nearly three months. The company I worked for had just hired Rick, and he was staying with us in our guest room until the school year was over and his wife and children could join him. Rick was a wonderful guy, but he tended toward shyness, especially around strangers.

One night, Bobbie and I were going out to meet friends for dinner, so we left Missy and Julie—then 14 and 11—home to eat dinner with Rick. Scared that they would sit there staring silently at each other for an hour or so, the girls came to me for help.

Fortunately, I remembered the tennis ball illustration. "I want you to picture yourself sitting at the table with Rick," I told them. "He won't be able to see the stack of tennis balls you've hidden in your laps.

After you say the blessing for dinner, I want one of you—Julie, you go first—to reach down, pick up one of the tennis balls, and throw it to Rick."

Knowing from experience that good table manners were important to me, they looked shocked. "Dad," Missy exclaimed, "you're not serious."

After just a moment of making them think I really meant for this dinner to turn into Wimbledon, I assured them I was kidding. "Well, kind of," I finally said.

I told them about the game of conversation. "When you want to talk with people, you *throw* them a question, just like a tennis ball. And, hopefully, they'll *catch* it and *throw* it back with an answer. You catch the ball and throw another question back.

"Of course," I explained, "you never actually tell anyone you're playing a game of catch. You keep that to yourself."

This was beginning to sound like fun, eating dinner and playing a game at the same time. I explained that "tennis balls" may be questions like "Who was your favorite teacher when you were in grade school? Who was your best friend in junior high? What sports did you like when you were growing up?"

"What if Rick doesn't throw the ball back?" Missy alertly asked.

"That's okay, Missy," I said. "If he doesn't return the ball, just throw him another one."

The girls were ready for dinner—and Rick.

Bobbie and I got home late that night. The report of tennis balls at dinnertime would have to wait for a few more hours. However, the next morning, our two girls were bursting with the news of the previous night's dinner. "How did it go?" I asked.

Missy's eyes were wide. "Dad," she said, "it went great. By the time we were finished with dinner, Rick was *covered* with tennis balls!"

I laughed and celebrated. This was big.

Teach your girl how to carry on a conversation. Role-play and practice. Teach her to listen so she can ask a question that follows what you've just said. Show her how it works.

"Tell me about your recess today at school, Julie," I'd say to start the rehearsal.

"Brandon fell off the monkey bars," she'd say.

"Wow, did he hurt himself?"

"I think so."

"How do you know?"

"He cried."

"What did Mrs. Bond do?"

"She took Brandon to the school nurse."

"Then what happened?"

"The nurse called Brandon's mother."

"I'll bet you felt sorry for Brandon . . ."

The secret of an effective conversation is to never just stick the ball in your pocket. If, after Julie had told me that Brandon had cracked his head on the playground, I had only said, "That's too bad" or "I'm sorry for Brandon," I would have been putting the ball in my pocket. Instead, however, I threw it back with a question: "Wow, did he hurt himself?"

Forgive me if going through this elementary exercise is insulting to your intelligence, but I know that your natural tendency will be to stick tennis balls in your pocket. And if you do, you'll miss the opportunities that present themselves to show your little girl exactly how to make a conversation work.

"That's a Pretty Picture, Honey"

Little children are famous for indecipherable drawings. But instead of saying, "That's nice, sweetie" or "What is it?" you need to say, "Tell me about your picture, Jennifer."

Then Jennifer describes what *she* sees, which, of course, is all that matters. As she talks, you listen—carefully—so you can say, "It's so interesting that you colored the pony orange. Can you tell me how you chose that pretty color?"

Your girl is learning to speak, to accurately express what's inside. And you're learning to listen so you can catch a glimpse of who this little girl really is.

Then when Jennifer comes home from high school after a verbal bout with one of her classmates, you say, "Tell me about Mindy." Listen carefully. Next, follow up with genuine sympathy—something like, "I'm sorry that Mindy said something so mean. I'm sure it really hurt when she said that."

Fortunately, a 16-year-old Jennifer will talk to you that way because, when she was small and the stakes weren't as high, you taught her how.

"It's Nice to Meet You, Dr. Holland"

Our home in Waco, Texas, was a full 100 miles from a major airport. Because my work required a lot of travel, I was forced to fly a commuter plane between Waco and Dallas.

It was one of those ancient planes where there was no door between the cockpit and the passengers . . . and no, Wilbur Wright was not the pilot's name. Anyway, for the most part, I prefer not knowing what's actually going on up there, just as I'd rather not know what really happens in a restaurant kitchen. But in this case, there was no choice.

Fastened to the flight yoke with a thick rubber band was a laminated card. At the top of the card were the words *Preflight Checklist*. Before the plane left its moorings in front of the terminal, the passengers got a look at the captain as he went down his checklist, making sure he hadn't forgotten anything.

Less than a century ago, children were taught the art of conversation in school. They were given a checklist of how to talk—what to say, what not to say, how to greet an adult, and the use of the words *sir* and *ma'am*. But most schools today won't provide your girl with such a checklist, so you're going to have to do it yourself.

Today's lesson is on meeting grown-ups. Remember, this isn't going to happen properly without some instruction—a checklist to fasten to her mind with a "thick rubber band."

You begin this lesson by telling your daughter that there will be times when you'll want to introduce her to your friends. You remind her that she's important to you, and you want your friends to meet such a special girl.

Then you describe a typical situation. You're out with her, and one of your friends walks up to the two of you. This happens a lot on weekends—at grocery stores and Home Depot—since you've taken your girl with you on all your errands. You say to your friend, "Hey, Gary, have you met Julie?"

"No, I don't believe I have," your friend answers.

You look at your little girl and say these words: "Julie, I'd like you to meet my friend, Dr. Holland. Dr. Holland, this is Julie."

Julie looks at Gary Holland—not at his shoes but at his *eyes*—holds out her hand, and says, "It's nice to meet you, Dr. Holland."

Gary, without any prompting from you, will take her hand, shake it, and faint, out cold on the floor. No, actually, he'll lean over, take her hand, and say something like, "Well, it's nice to meet you, too, Julie. You're such a delightful little girl."

You may be saying, "Come on. This sounds awfully rigid. After all, we're not living in Victorian England. I prefer letting my daughter be her spontaneous little self."

Okay, but you're missing a golden opportunity to give your girl the gift of esteem that comes from receiving an adult's approval. If you follow this plan, she gets to hear a grown-up's kind words of affirmation, the reassurance that she *is* a special girl, from someone—a big person—she's just met.

I encourage you to practice this one until she gets it right. And if she slips up in an actual meeting, take the opportunity—once Dr. Holland is no longer around—to correct the mistakes. Be sure to affirm the parts she got right: "That was good, honey, but you forgot to look right at Dr. Holland when you put out your hand and said, 'Nice to meet you, Dr. Holland.' The next time, look at his eyes when you're speaking to him."

WHAT WAS YOUR FAVORITE THING TODAY?

If you and your wife have more than one child, you'll discover that conversational ability is stronger in some children than in others. Your older daughter may be more deliberate in her talking, making each of her words count. Your younger child may be spontaneous and talkative, never leaving you to wonder what she's thinking. Family conversations may be lopsided, with one child completely dominating—maybe she'll run for city council someday and make you proud—and the other holding back.

Bobbie invented a way to create balanced table conversation when the girls were small. She would routinely suggest that we "go around the table and tell each other our happiest thing and our saddest thing today."

No one was exempt. I had to talk about my day along with everyone else. From the girls, we heard about neighborhood toughs and hurt feelings. We listened to each report. One summer, for almost a month, Julie's happiest thing was the neighbor's new sliding board. And we did our best to listen as though we had never heard about it before.

Our friends Henry and Marilynn Blackaby told us something they had done with their family at dinnertime when their kids were young. "What did God say to you today?" they'd ask each child. Throughout their day, the Blackaby children would be on the lookout for "God sightings," and then they'd enthusiastically report these to their family that night over a meal. What a wonderful idea.

These times of good talk with your children are the stuff with which relationships are built. And they should be guarded as though they were priceless. Difficult as it is to coordinate your schedules to have dinner together, I strongly encourage you to fight for it—two or three times a week, minimum.

Julie and Christopher took table conversation into a new dimension with our granddaughters Harper and Ella. Sometimes during a meal, someone had something to say that they did not want to be repeated to anyone. Anywhere. Not for any reason at all.

When something like that was introduced, they would say, "Okay, this is 'club talk.'" And then everyone at the table knew that under no conditions—even the threat of torture—could any of this be repeated outside the circle. Whether the subject was sex or Santa, "club talk" was a family secret.

By the way, "club talk" didn't include heated arguments between Mom and Dad. When they told me about this part, Christopher and Julie said that confidential table talk could include "processing" tough issues, but if the temperature started to rise and a fight was rearing its nasty head, a temporary truce was made and that part was finished later, one-on-one.

Speaking of conversation, you're going to discover—if you haven't already—that electronic gadgets provide your family members with a choice. "Talk to each other or gaze at your little screen in your hands." It's not uncommon to see a family seated around a restaurant table, each with their own little device. This is a lost opportunity for conversation.

We have a good friend who has gone so far as to place a small wicker basket near her front door. A little sign, tastefully lettered, rests inside the basket. "Welcome to our home. Thank you for leaving your cell phone here." (She also suggests that the ringers be turned off so their time together isn't interrupted by choruses of annoying chirps and beeps.) During mealtime, everyone in the family is asked to place their cell phone in the basket. This is a good idea.

SHELLING LIMA BEANS, SHUCKING CORN, AND DOING THE DISHES

A chapter about conversation would be unnecessary if this book had been published a hundred years ago. Working together as a family was the perfect setting for good talk.

My personal ancestry traces to Lancaster County, Pennsylvania. Even if you have never been there, you've probably at least seen pictures of horses and buggies, of bonneted women, and of little boys with "bowl" haircuts and straw hats.

I have sweet memories of my extended family during summer visits when I was a youngster. Although my uncles and aunts' farms had electricity and running water, they did not have any televisions. They also didn't have dishwashers. Not only were mealtimes rich with good conversation, but also preparing for these meals and cleaning up afterward were natural settings for talking. Without any effort, I can shuttle my memory to a circle of lawn chairs in the front yard, yanking reluctant husks from sweet corn and brushing off the silk threads. I also remember cracking open the green jackets that encased lima beans and spilling out the little jewels into shiny bowls that made a little dinging sound when they hit the sides. After meals we would stand in the kitchen together and towel off the dishes.

And you know what we did with each other during these chores? Yes. We talked nonstop. Everyone worked. Everyone chatted. Everyone connected.

Of course, I'm not advocating that your family do these same chores. (Besides, you may be open to shelling lima beans but feeling nauseous at the thought of actually eating them.) However, I am suggesting that working together on a project—the more mundane, the better—can be a wonderful opportunity for conversation. Projects like folding laundry, sweeping out the garage, or painting a fence together on a mission project come to mind. Conversations can flow seamlessly when you're doing stuff together.

When we lived in Nashville, I occasionally had long conversations with my friend and neighbor Dale Jamison. Sometimes these talks would last for a solid hour. Sometimes more. "I thought women were the ones who did this kind of thing," you might be saying, and of course you'd be right. What I didn't mention is that my conversations with Dale often took place while jogging along Middle Tennessee's country roads. Working together can create a lovely platform for talk.

A Pile of Rocks and Other Important Memories

In the Old Testament, the story is told of Jacob on his way to find a wife. In the night, he had an encounter with an angel. Without going into detail here, let's just say it was a serious conversation! The next morning, as Jacob was preparing to break camp and move on, he decided to build a little monument—a simple pile of rocks—to that conversation.

Although it's not recorded, I wouldn't be surprised if when Jacob returned home with Rachel on his arm, he passed by that pile of rocks and told his bride about the night he spent talking with an angel.

There's a restaurant in Waco that will, for all our lives, be a pile of rocks for Missy, Julie, and me. Harold Waite's was one of those old-time diners where the burgundy-vinyl-covered booth benches were repaired with gray duct tape, the imitation walnut Formica on the tables was worn to white at the edges, smokers were everywhere, and the waitress called you "Honey." She could refill your coffee cup in an instant from a distance without spilling a drop. It was a place where, maybe twice a month for the five years we lived in Texas, the three of us would have Saturday morning breakfast together.

And because there are still restaurants like that all over America (except for the smoking part), every time Missy and Julie see an old diner, they remember our Saturday breakfasts and talks. To them it's like Jacob's pile of rocks.

DOTS OVER BREAKFAST

One of the dangers of such breakfast meetings is that you may have a hard time finding things to talk about, especially *before* your scrambled eggs and their French toast arrive. In fact, when you and your girl find your special place, you may see other dads—who have been to a seminar or read a book about the importance of doing this—with their children. Sometimes, if you look closely, you may see dads fingering their smartphones on their laps or watching cable news on the TV hanging from the ceiling in the corner of the restaurant.

Flag on the play. Fifteen-yard penalty.

The last thing you want your girl to recall about this special place is sitting there bored to death while you read your messages or checked the scores from last night's games.

What we did was play Dots. You might remember playing this game when you were a kid. You take a piece of paper and lay out a series of dots in rows and columns.

Each of you takes a turn connecting two dots, either horizontally or vertically.

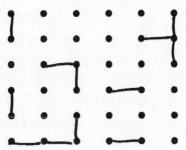

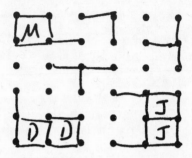

The trick is to be able to complete a box with your line. And when you do, you put your initial inside the box. Every time you write your initial, you get to connect two more dots. The most initials when all the possible lines are drawn wins.

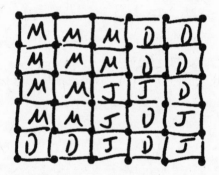

You can come up with another game, but this one was great fun for us, and it didn't make any annoying electronic sounds!

The important thing is that it gave us something to do every time we went out to breakfast. While we were connecting dots, we would talk. Finally—and please don't miss this one—it was the only time we ever played Dots. There were other times when we were tempted to get out a piece of paper and play Dots, but we resisted the temptation. Dots was a sacrament, only for Harold Waite's. In fact, the girls eventually started calling our breakfast place Harold Dots. The game was another rock pile that will, for the rest of the girls' lives, represent one simple thing: good conversation.

FOR GIRLS ONLY?

You may be wondering, especially if you also have a son, "Isn't it important to teach a boy how to talk too?"

Yes, of course it is. However, there are several reasons why I place such importance on conversation between you and your daughter. Among these is the fact that, for the most part, girls have the capacity of becoming more adept at conversation than boys at an early age. Since you're being a good conversation instructor for her, she will teach others—especially boys—how to do the same. As she begins to discover the world of other men besides you, she'll be able to make better judgments about who's compatible as a potential friend and who's not.

As she begins to discover the world of other men besides you, she'll be able to make better judgments about who's compatible as a potential friend and who's not.

As she throws "tennis balls" at boys, she'll learn who they are and what's important to them. She will be less likely to be surprised by a boy's errant belief system or broken moral compass if she has been engaged in meaningful conversation with him.

Because she has learned the art of good conversation, your daughter will be aware that talking to someone in person and text messaging are not equals. One is authentic. The other—all 140 characters—can be quite synthetic.

When our granddaughter turned 16 and was finally able to date (Jon, her daddy, is brilliant), she received a text message from a boy—a good friend of hers from church—asking her to go to the prom. Abby was not impressed with his cowardly approach to the invitation in a text message and answered with one word: "No."

The boy was crushed. He also got the real message. So being a young man with plenty of courage, determination, and creativity, he tried again. He called Abby's mom, our daughter Missy, and asked if he could come to their house to meet with Abby. Missy asked Abby, she agreed, and a time was set.

A talented musician, the young man brought his guitar and met Abby on the driveway in front of her house. He also brought flowers and a folding chair so he could sit down for his serenade. Although no one in our family remembers all the lyrics to the song—because Abby told us about it—we do remember that the song included:

I'd like a second chance,
To ask you to the dance.
So I called your mom
And I'd like to take you to the prom . . .

This time, Abby said yes.

As wonderful and effective as electronic communication is, there is not—nor will there ever be—anything to replace the wonder of speaking (or in this case, singing) face-to-face.

Please Fasten Your Seat Belt

Every day in America, there are more than 87 thousand airplane flights. Just over 30 thousand of these are commercial—American, Southwest, Delta, United. There are just about the same number of "general aviation" flights—private planes. And there are about 25 thousand "air taxi" flights . . . charters (think professional and college sports teams), military, and cargo flights. At any given daylight moment, there are over five thousand airplanes in the sky, and in a single year, air traffic controllers handle approximately 64 million takeoffs and landings.

If what I just said about electronic versus in-person relationships were not true, (except for overnight packages) the airline business would dry up.

Think about it. You and I go through all the hassle of flying—a lot more hassle since September 11, 2001—in order to do one thing: See someone and speak with him or her. Of course, cell phones and computer-based video connections are terrific. But we have figured out that, in truth, these fall short. It's worth the cost to zoom around the country on airplanes just so we can actually be with each other . . . customers, family, friends. Every day, two and a half million of us put our seat backs and tray tables in the upright position just so we can actually see each other say, "Hello."[1]

TAKING WORDS BACK

This chapter opened with a painful lesson I learned about the power of words. As adults, you and I know that once something has been spoken, it simply cannot be retrieved.

Listening to talk radio is a good reminder of this. The host's microphone is live. When something is spoken, it shoots out on the airwaves and cannot be pulled back. It's toothpaste squeezed from a tube. It can never be replaced.

But you can always tell professionals from amateurs on the radio by how they deal with mistakes. An amateur will catch himself, issue a few uhs and ums, and then fall all over himself apologizing for having said the wrong thing. He may even nervously laugh at what he has done.

A professional will quickly acknowledge the mistake, fix it, and then go on: "The Chicago Bears scored three touchdowns in the second inning, rather, the second *quarter,* of their battle with the Green Bay Packers."

Even as a seasoned conversationalist, you're going to make mistakes. You're going to say foolish and inappropriate things. Don't ignore them. But don't grovel and blubber, either.

Acknowledge your blunder, admit it, correct it, and move on with the conversation. Getting good at this will help you teach your girl how to do the same thing when she fails.

THE IMPORTANCE OF SAYING "I'M SORRY"

Because Julie was old enough to push the lawn mower, my weeklong business trip and the ankle-deep grass surrounding our house gave her all she needed to decide to surprise me.

Driving home from the airport, I was reviewing the chores waiting at home. *My grass must be knee-deep by now. I certainly hope none of the neighbor kids has gotten lost in my front yard.*

But when I pulled into the driveway, I couldn't believe what I was seeing. Someone had *already* cut the grass, and it looked pretty good. I say "pretty good" because I have this thing about my lawn. My goal is to have it look like a major-league infield. In addition to collecting the clippings, I crosshatch my mowing at a perfect 45-degree angle, alternating the direction each time I cut it. I also slice along the grass next to the driveway and flower beds with my edge trimmer. It looks like my freshly waxed high-school flattop the whole way around.

Whoever had mowed my yard hadn't caught the clippings or edged around the beds. Here and there were clumps of cut grass. Don't get me wrong; I was glad someone had taken the initiative to do the yard. It's just that it wasn't exactly the way I would have done it.

When I walked into the house, I could tell immediately that it was Julie who had mowed the lawn. She had that "Aren't you proud of me?" look all over her face. I hugged her and thanked her for doing such a thoughtful thing. I didn't say a thing about the loose clumps of grass or the scraggly edges. I was so proud of my verbal restraint. But I did change immediately into my work clothes and go outside to *recut* the grass . . . properly.

When Julie looked outside to see what I was doing, she was

crushed. Although I had *said* nothing about my displeasure, what I *did* that summer afternoon spoke volumes. My perfectionistic foolishness had crushed my daughter's spirit.

That evening, Bobbie took me aside to tell me how Julie had reacted. The pain that my silent criticism had inflicted on her was far worse than a little extra thatch in my grass or unmanicured edges.

In my haste to get it just right, I had missed a chance to celebrate my daughter's honest attempt to please her dad. And I had hurt her feelings in the process. Finally realizing that, I went to her, said I was sorry, and asked for her pardon. Fortunately, she forgave me for being such an insensitive boob.

When you blow it with your daughter, as I did, be quick to repent and apologize. "I'm sorry, Julie. I was wrong. Will you please forgive me?"

A Lesson from a Jackhammer

Believe it or not, the first time I used a jackhammer, I learned a key lesson about the importance of conversation.

The thing that drives a jackhammer is air under tremendous pressure. This pressurized air comes from a compressor that, with the help of a gasoline engine, fills a tank to which a hose from the jackhammer is connected. You've seen contractors pulling these compressors around behind their pickups.

When the tank is filling with air, you can hear the gas engine running full speed. But when the tank is full, the engine seems to slip into neutral, and you can hear a loud hissing sound. This sound comes from a small valve attached to the air tank. What it does is simple: When the tank is packed tightly with air, so tightly that any more air would blow up the whole thing, sending the entire crew to that great coffee break in the sky, that pressure valve tells the engine to rest, and then it releases some of the air.

That little, inexpensive pressure valve preserves an expensive piece of equipment and the lives of the people working close by. What a nice idea.

Conversation does the same thing. Used properly, it can release the pressure that builds in every relationship. It's that magic little device that gives people the opportunity to talk about frustrations or fears without allowing pressure to build, expensive "compressors" to explode, and people to be seriously harmed.

Give your daughter the gift of conversation.

Builder's Checklist

Conversation is absolutely foundational in your relationship with your daughter. But it won't happen automatically. Here are a few reminders from this chapter:

1. *Show your daughter that words are wonderful.* Read to your girl even before you think she can understand a thing. It will create in her a love for words and an appreciation for your bringing the world to her through books.

2. *Engage in honoring conversation.* Don't let your daughter interrupt when you're in a conversation with someone else. This includes when you're on the phone. When she interrupts, get her attention, and remind her that you're speaking with someone else. Then when you're finished with your conversation, get back to her right away and find out what she wanted to talk about.

3. *Stay on top of electronics.* This is a big one, but you can do it. Remember that technology is primarily a tool, not a toy. Using it to search for information is a marvel. But when it becomes a toy, then most personal interaction stops. Make these gadgets work for you.

4. *Take her along.* Try not to run any errands without your girl next to you in the front seat. While you're riding along, get

conversation started with questions about her surroundings: "How many cows?" "How many buses?" It's easy.

5. *Play verbal tennis.* Teach your girl how conversation works. Throw her a question and teach her how to throw back a response. Try to avoid sticking the ball in your pocket too soon. Also, be sure to listen carefully.

6. *Ask good questions.* Instead of saying, "That's nice, sweetie," try "Tell me about your picture" or "What an interesting combination you're wearing. Tell me why you chose such an unusual outfit."

7. *Teach her to say, "It's nice to meet you, Dr. Holland."* Teach your daughter how to properly meet someone. Practice until she gets it right.

8. *Please pass the conversation.* Don't be so quick to excuse your daughter from the dinner table. Expect her to stay and contribute to the conversation, or just to listen. Be careful to include her as much as possible so it's not too painful! This might be a good time to ask, "What was your favorite thing today?"

9. *Pile up the rocks.* Look for places to call your own: an old diner in your town for breakfast or a city park for walking. It doesn't have to be fancy or expensive; it just needs to be.

10. *Apologize for words poorly spoken and inconsiderate actions.* Because you're normal, you're going to say or do the wrong thing at the wrong time. You're going to hurt people's feelings, including your daughter's. Show her what it sounds like to hear her dad correct his words and actions, and, if necessary, ask her forgiveness for the error. "I'm sorry. I was wrong. Will you please forgive me?"

11. *Realize that all this will take time and patience.* But the rewards of having a girl grow up to be one of your best friends are incredible. And conversation is how this relationship will grow.

AFFECTION

Daddy, Hold Me

> *Praise is well, compliment is well, but*
> *affection—that is the last and final and most*
> *precious reward that any man can win.*
> —MARK TWAIN

Biology was my favorite subject in high school. It was the only class I had where I could do something with my hands other than taking notes or turning pages. Foolishly, I didn't take any "shop" classes in high school.

I remember what it felt like walking into Wesley Dusek's biology classroom at the Wheaton Community High School. If I take a deep breath, I can still remember the odor—not Mr. Dusek, but the formaldehyde and various other chemicals. Standing in the doorway in my memory, I can see the lab tables to my left, the huge black countertop with a sink in the middle of it, and the blackboard to my right.

At the right end of the blackboard hung a huge, life-sized, full-color flip chart of a naked man. He didn't even have his skin on. This chart had several pages of transparent overlays, each illustrating one of the systems inside the man. There was the skeletal system, the respiratory system, the digestive system, the reproductive system (our favorite—we were sophomore boys), and the nervous system.

Maybe you had a chart like that in your biology class too.

If you did, can you remember what the nervous system looked like? It showed the brain, which looked like cold oatmeal with deep wrinkles, the spinal column, and all the nerves coming out from it that looked like little rivers and streams.

Question: Where was the largest congregation of nerves once they'd left the spinal column? In other words, where was the biggest collection of nerves that would make for the highest degree of sensitivity?

Right. It was in the hands and fingers.

THE POWER OF TOUCH

In fact, although you'll never find this on any chart, it almost seems as if there's so much feeling in the hands and fingers that there ought to be a little connector—a nerve, a blood vessel, or maybe a clear plastic tube—between the hands and the heart. This is especially true for a woman.

Way back at the beginning of the Old Testament, in the first chapter of Genesis, we have the record of God creating the heavens and the earth by speaking them into existence. Four times during that week, God summarized His work with the words "it was good." And on the sixth day, the day He created a human, His work is described as "very good."

To your daughter, touching is the key to her heart.

Imagine what it would have been like to be Adam. God had set him in a pristine and perfect place, surrounding him with luscious vegetation and animals of every description. Life every day for Adam was like the flawless Sunday afternoon.

Because I'm a dog guy, I have pictured the first man fearlessly tussling with the animals in his garden. Can't you see him stroking the fur of some really big creatures and having them return his affection with a yawn and a purr? But as he surveyed his surroundings and the beauty that he found there, a sinking feeling crept into his being. Because he had been soaking in perfection, this was a new sensation. A "not good" feeling.

What could this mean? Adam must have thought.

Because you and I are familiar with this story, we know what happens next. If we take ourselves back to the spot where Adam had this epiphany, we know for sure what was missing. We understand this sinking in his heart.

Adam was a man without . . . a woman.

So God invited Adam to take a nap. Taking a rib from Adam's side, God fashioned another living thing. When he awoke, Adam saw something more remarkable than he had ever seen before. It was a creature that stood upright as he did. It had arms and legs, but that's where the similarity ended. And it wasn't only her body that was different; there was something mysterious and unexplainable. Wonderful. Because men love to name stuff, Adam called her "woman" . . . because she had been taken from him.[1]

Immediately following this scene is a sentence in the Bible that reads like an editorial insertion. "This explains why a man leaves his father and mother and is joined to his wife, and the two are united into one."[2] In a flash, we transition from the physique of a being to a relationship with her. From the tangible to the intangible.

But this sentence is not out of context. It's there on purpose. For in that moment, you and I are introduced to our other half. The "not good" that Adam had experienced was the "not good" of being incomplete. The woman wasn't simply another fixture in Adam's critter collection; this was someone with whom he would connect. Look at the sentence again. The words are "joined" and "united."

One aspect of this connecting is physical. With a sparkle in your eye, it's how your daughter came to be. But there's another dimension to this that won't make a baby, even though it's no less important. This is the emotional melding power of touch—especially for a woman. Your wife. And your daughter.

Here's what I'm talking about. Please do not miss this. In the next chapter of the Bible, when the serpent was trying to get Eve to disobey God by picking and eating the forbidden fruit, she told Satan that God had commanded Adam not even to *touch* the fruit.[3]

You can look for yourself, but God never told Adam not to touch the fruit. He only told him not to eat it.[4] But to Eve—a woman— *touching* the fruit was just the same as picking it and eating it.

To your daughter, touching is the key to her heart. And, as you'll see, there are two kinds of touching you'll use with your girl: physical and verbal.

A STOUT WARNING

As you read the rest of this chapter, your mind will naturally be drawn to an important issue. Touching your daughter falls into two categories: appropriate physical and verbal touching and *inappropriate* physical and verbal touching.

Tragically, the news reports constantly remind us that there are fathers—and predatory teachers and coaches and others—who don't know the difference. We see photos of them being shamefully ushered off to prison where they belong. We hear horrific accounts from grown women who are dealing with the unthinkable trauma of having been violated by fathers—or father figures—who disregarded their own consciences.

If you're afraid you may be such a father, please stop reading this book and seek the help of a trained professional.

PHYSICAL TOUCHING

So if you're still reading, you know the difference between appropriate and inappropriate touching. And if I could sit down with you right now and look into your eyes, I'd tell you not to miss what follows. No, I'd beg you not to miss it.

Hold your daughter when she's a baby, and gently stroke her face. Hold her hand when you walk with her. Visit her room just before she goes to sleep, and kiss her good night. Hug her with your whole arms; wrap her up like a blanket. Let her heart know—through that little connector between her toucher and her heart—that she is absolutely secure in her daddy's arms.

All this takes some extra time. You cannot do any of this meaningful touching on the run. You have to slow down to make it mean something.

ROCK AROUND THE CLOCK

Both of my maternal grandparents and my paternal grandmother lived their final years in a retirement center in south-central Pennsylvania called Messiah Village. The first time we visited the "rest home," the director took us on a tour. The decor was tasteful, and the staff seemed professional and good natured.

What I'll never forget was a large room we walked into. Probably measuring 20 by 50 feet, it was literally filled with rocking chairs. The director explained that there was a day care center for preschoolers right in the middle of the home. The playground was in the atrium surrounded by the residents' rooms, so throughout the day, the voices of children wafted through the complex.

Each day, right after lunch, it was quiet time for the kids. They would file into this large, rocking-chair-filled room, looking for their special friend. Crawling up on their adopted lap, they would experience the touch—and, therefore, the love—of an elderly person with lots of it to give.

"Visiting this room during quiet time is an awesome thing," the director explained. "The room is intentionally darkened, and the shadowed back-and-forth squeak of the rockers and soft sounds of talking or humming make it feel like a holy place. It's almost like standing in the hushed chancel of a great European cathedral."

The Nobel Prize for good ideas goes to the person who came up with this one.

Eavesdropping on that scene would probably turn up little in the way of lectures about life. You would not have heard, "Actually, I tend to vote for the most conservative candidate, since . . ." or "You know, I'm glad you asked me that question, because . . ." But the power of touch was wrapping itself into the souls of those little children, assuring them they were worthy of someone's love, that life need not be frightening, that good is stronger than evil, and that love is best communicated in a touch.

All the airplane travel I mentioned in the last chapter isn't only about talking to each other face-to-face; it's about touching, too. I can get a lump in my throat right now, thinking about the happy reunions I have seen played out in airports. And, in every case, touching is involved.

Hold your daughter. Stop running, take a minute, and touch your girl.

On the Road Again

In the summer of 1978, I started running for exercise. I had been on the track team in junior high, but in the intervening years, I had lost my interest in the sport. Jim Fixx had just published *The Complete Book of Running*; shoemakers were beginning to discover that there was more to life than low-cut Converse All-Stars. I bought a pair of expensive running shoes and was off.

In 1992, when we moved to our Tennessee house, tucked among a few foothills, I found a wonderful five-and-a-half-mile winding road that encircled our neighborhood. It provided just enough terrain and scenery to make it interesting, but not so much that I'd become discouraged by its difficulty.

The only thing I didn't like about this run was the dog living between miles three and four. He was a husky, gray with electric blue eyes and mean—very angry and threatening. Sometimes he'd be standing on the road as I approached. At other times he'd be hiding behind a tree or a barn, just waiting to charge me, barking and snarling as if I were some specially flavored dog treat.

I hated this dog. I plotted his demise. I thought of driving up the road late some night and shooting his lights out with a shotgun. Then I decided to buy a can of Mace. *Yes, I can spray the Mace in his eyes, and he'll never chase me again. I'll get that vicious animal. I'll teach him who's boss around these hills.*

But before I had a chance to buy the Mace, I bumped into the guy who lived at the end of our street. Although we had never run together, I knew he was a runner too. I asked if he knew about "my" five-and-a-half-mile course. He said he did. I asked if he knew about the husky. He said he did. I asked if the dog had frightened him the way he frightened me. He said, "Well, at first he did."

"At first?" I returned.

"Yes, until one day I decided to stop running for a moment. I had put some dog biscuits in the pocket of my running shorts, so I squatted down in the middle of the road and gave him one. The dog licked my hand and rolled over on his back, begging me to scratch the nether regions of his tummy. Now I look forward to seeing him when I run."

I felt so stupid. This "angry" dog just wanted a friend, someone to stop running long enough to stroke his fur and pat his head.

Stop running and touch your daughter. Touching connects. Touching seals a peace. Touching is like glue bonding you together for the rest of your lives.

When you take your daughter along with you in your car on those weekend errands, every once in a while reach over and pat her knee. Don't make it a big deal; just touch her. When you're sitting next to her in church, gently squeeze her hand. You don't even need to look at her. In fact, this squeeze will be like a little silent conversation. Just between you and her.

SECRET CONNECTIONS

My mother taught us something her mother had taught her—kind of a "squeeze" language. The way it works is that you take your daughter's hand—church is a great place for this—and tenderly squeeze it four times in a row. Then she squeezes your hand three times. You return the three squeezes with two of your own. She ends this silent conversation with one final strong squeeze of your hand.

The interpretation of this squeezing conversation is "Do you love me?" Four words, four squeezes. Her answer is, "Yes, I do." Three words, three squeezes. Your response is, "How much?" And her final answer comes in a strong squeeze.

You might be thinking, *Come on. Isn't this a little silly—touching, patting, squeezing? "Talking" in squeeze language? Couldn't I just buy her something?*

No, it's not only *not* silly, but it may even be one of the sweetest things you and your daughter will share. It will be something you'll never outgrow. It may be the only "words" you'll be able to speak at awkward or painful moments. And the older *you* get, the more love you'll feel in touches coming *from* your daughter. Of course, she will have learned this from you.

And it never gets old. Missy is in her forties, and the last time we sat next to each other in church, we held hands . . . and squeezed.

THE FALL OF THE WALL

In the mid-1980s, when the Berlin Wall was about to crumble, I saw a news account of East Germans boarding a train to visit friends and family living in West Germany. As the train pulled away from the station, thousands of people who had boarded the train were throwing money out the window. I can still see thousands of swirling bills following the train as it wound its way to freedom.

Why were they doing such a foolish thing? Why would anyone throw their money away?

It was simple. These were East German marks, and there was no longer an East Germany. Where these people were going, their money no longer worked.

Too often, in their genuine attempts to demonstrate affection to their daughters, dads buy them things. "I'm not too good at this gentleness stuff, so I'll go splurge a little and show her how much I really care."

Sorry, but though that strategy sounds very logical—maybe because it worked with you!—it doesn't work with your daughter. The cherished place you want your relationship with her to go doesn't use that "currency."

Your daughter is far more interested in you—your time and your gentle affection—than she is in any stuff you could buy her.

Rub-a-Dub-Dub

One of the gifts I gave my wife when the girls were small was taking responsibility for giving baths. Once they had outgrown the kitchen sink, leaning over the bathtub became my job. Actually, it wasn't that bad.

I remember sliding them back and forth in the slippery tub, pretending they were hockey pucks. I can picture little "hats" we made with the soapsuds. I can feel the weight of Missy's or Julie's head in my hand as I washed each girl's hair under the stream of water coming from the spigot. "It isn't too hot, is it?" I always gave them a washcloth to hold over their eyes to make it as painless as possible.

As I lifted them out of the tub, they would kick the excess water from their feet. Then standing them in front of me as I sat on the closed commode, I towel-dried their slippery bodies and wet hair.

Although I initially thought of this job as a chore, looking back on it now, I realize it was a gift to me, too—to have the privilege of making a dad's touch as normal as breathing and sleeping. Touching inextricably bonded my daughters to me and me to them.

How old is your daughter before she lets you know she's too old for her daddy to give her a bath? She *will* let you know. This communiqué may come as early as when she's three or four years old. It may not happen until she's five or six. She may tell your wife. Or you may detect a glimmer of unfamiliar shyness or even shame. When it happens, you're done with bathing her. That's okay. The fun experience has deposited plenty of tender security in your daughter's memory bank.

A couple of final words about touching:

First, when your daughter draws closer to her teenage years, you may go through a time of anxiety about showing physical affection. Your girl is becoming a woman, and her body is changing shape. It almost feels like she's pulling back from you. You used to be her go-to guy for hugs and advice. Now she goes to her mom. Or her friends.

Boys may become part of her dinnertime conversation. This boy is cute and that boy makes her laugh. This boy is very cool and all the girls like that boy. You used to be the cute and funny and cool boy. Not so much anymore.

Even though this phase may be a little painful for you, I encourage you not to take it personally. It's a tunnel. She'll eventually come out the other side. In the meantime, be yourself. Don't act hurt or withdraw from her. Your daughter will be back in no time.

Second, do not use touching to get something from your daughter. It won't work. If you try to touch or hold her after you've wronged her in some way or when you're in a conflict, she'll yank back from you. She has a right to do that.

Touching works only when you've talked out a tough situation or when things are in good shape between you and her. Touching is the signature scrawled at the end of an agreement to seal it. Touching is not a scheme to get your way.

Done right, it's a connector that has no expiration date.

TOUCHING WITH YOUR WORDS

Touching words—statements of affection—seal the contract that physical touch writes. Words define exactly what it is you're thinking or feeling. They leave no room for doubt.

These words can be written or spoken. My wife taught me about this a long time ago.

When the girls were in grade school, Bobbie packed their lunches every day. In each girl's brown bag, Bobbie always included a small luncheon napkin. *On* the napkin, she'd write a note. Every day she would say something special. It could have been as general as "I love you today," or as specific as "I'm praying that you do well on your science test."

The girls regularly told us that their friends would ask, "What did your mom write today?" These written "touchings" made the girls proud. Occasionally, Bobbie would ask me to write the napkin message for the day, but I can't take any credit for this great idea. It was all hers.

Note: If you have a son, and you or your wife pack his lunch, don't do napkin notes. This is not a good idea for boys. I won't go into the whys of this admonition; you'll just have to trust me.

Early on, we learned the fun of leaving notes everywhere. Notes left on pillows and tucked into shoes and suitcases are powerful word touchings. Three- or four-word text messages in the middle of the day have the same strong impact. Please don't go on and on. Just, "I love you today" or "You're the best" will do. And don't take it personally if she doesn't reply. She read it and probably will delete it, but its impact will be tucked away in her heart.

> *The only way that word touchings work is if you have your daughter's undivided attention and you carefully speak each word.*

Just as physical touching takes a slowing-down moment, meaningful words take a little extra time too. If you're going to be serious about being successful with this one, you must learn to speak entire words and sentences.

For example, "Love ya, hon" doesn't qualify as a word touch. It's acceptable for your dog or tropical fish, but it's not going to work with your daughter. If you want to tell her you love her, say, "I love you." Then to seal it, say her name: "I love you, Vanessa." "I love you, Stephanie." "I love you, Katie."

Don't say it on the fly. Don't say "I love you" when you're trying to juggle your backpack, a cup of coffee, your jacket, and a bagel on your way out in the morning. Actually, you *can* do it this way, but it won't count the way it should. "I love you" is probably better than "Clean the garage, Jennifer" or "Don't pull the cat's tail, Allison," but it will score you no points.

The only way that word touchings work is if you have your daughter's undivided attention and you carefully speak each word.

If you have lots of children, you must take time to speak verbal affection to each one individually. Group word touchings are nice, but they, too, don't count for much. If you have a lot of kids and you try to single out one of them with a word touching, you know how difficult it is to hit the right name first. If you and your wife have cleverly titled all your children with names beginning with the same letter, you're getting what you deserve.

SING AND SCRATCH

No, the heading above does not refer to what many baseball players do during the national anthem. If you really want to have some fun with your girl, look for opportunities to *combine* verbal and physical touchings. There may be no better time for this than bedtime.

Picture sitting on the edge of your daughter's bed. She is lying on her stomach, and you're scratching her back. While you're doing that, you are speaking words like this: "You know, Tess, I was talking to some of my friends at work today. I was telling them about how proud I am of you. As I was driving home, I got to thinking that if I could pick a daughter from all the girls who have ever lived, I would pick you first."

Because my wife has a pretty singing voice, her verbal and physical duo included some songs along with the back scratching. The girls called it Sing and Scratch. It became an often-requested way to end our daughters' days. Think of it, multisensory affection poured out on little girls, sealing their knowledge of their parents' love for them.

There are three important don'ts to follow concerning verbal affection. Maybe these will be helpful to you:

1. Don't exaggerate. When you speak kind words to your girl, don't say things you both know are untrue. If you say, "You're the smartest girl in the whole world," your daughter will know, based on the experience of that day at school, that this is not true. It won't count. Don't even say, "You're the prettiest girl in the world." For the moment, that may be affirming to her, but in time, she'll realize it's not true. One glance at the magazines near the grocery checkout will overrule this one.

Instead, talk about your love for her. Say kind things that speak to your appreciation for her thoughtfulness or character.

2. Don't compliment other girls on things your daughter will never achieve. Let's say that you and your family are at your favorite restaurant. And let's say that another family comes into the restaurant, walking past you on the way to their table. Let's also say they have a girl who looks to be about the age of your daughter. And let's say that you utter something like, "Wow, look at that little girl's beautiful, curly, blonde hair."

Your daughter is sitting there with straight, mouse-brown hair. And until she's old enough to drive herself to a beauty salon, she's never going to have curly, blonde hair. (Actually, I wonder how many girls fix their hair to please their dads who always said nice things about other girls' hair.)

Or you might say, "Look how tall and slender that little girl is. I'll bet she's going to be a basketball player." Your daughter may already suspect that her legs will never be that long, and she'd rather paint a pretty picture than play basketball.

Instead of hearing something nice about another girl, your daughter will quickly realize she doesn't measure up. God didn't give her skinny legs and a tall physique. So she may stop eating, trying to please you by attempting to become something—or someone—she'll never be.

3. When you compliment her, don't add anything. Just stick to the issue. As your daughter is walking off the soccer field after a sound performance, simply tell her she did a good job. Don't add comments about how bad the other team was or how unfair the referee was. Don't tell her you love her because she did a good job. And remember, don't tell her she's a world-class soccer player. It doesn't count if you do. Just say that you could tell she did her best. That works.

If she helps with the dishes after a meal, thank her for being so thoughtful, and leave it at that. Don't say anything about how you used to help your mother before the age of dishwashers or how you helped with the laundry on the rocks down at the riverbank. Just thank her for her helpfulness. If you tell her she's the most thoughtful girl in the world, you'll need to keep her from finding out about people like Mother Teresa.

AFFECTION AND BOYS

As I've mentioned, when your daughter grows, you'll notice that she's noticing boys. The first time you hear her talking about them, you might get a little nervous. Thoughts of such a boy (monster) paying special attention to your girl and then attempting some form of affection on her may make you feel like throwing up.

When she turns 16 and begins to single date, you'll see her walking with a boy to his car, holding his hand. She may sit close to him on the couch. You'll probably feel sad or afraid.

Relax. Your "hedge" around her has been built with *your* loving touch and tender words. If a girl goes out with a boy, and her dad has *neglected* these things, then her need for physical and verbal affection will not have been satisfied. She'll be "looking for love," as an old Johnny Lee song warns, "in all the wrong places."

Fill her heart with a dad's love so that when she encounters a man with less nobility and virtue (and more active hormones), she won't be vulnerable to his advances. And because you've taught her how to talk to you, she'll tell you what happened out there. When the secrecy is taken away, your fear will subside. Don't be afraid to ask questions. Encourage her to set limits since, more often than not, the boy has his foot on the accelerator and your daughter has hers on the brake. Our girls—with the help of their mom—would have "the talk" with boys early in their dating relationship. They'd tell him that he can't touch her body and she won't touch his.

Teaching your daughter the art of conversation will go a long way toward protecting her with boys. Your girl will have the confidence and skill to say, "I'm sorry, that's unacceptable," rather than quietly acquiesce to a boy's advances. Making out usually begins when talking stops.

Keeping a Healthy Balance in Your Account

In his best-selling book *His Needs, Her Needs,* Dr. Willard Harley offers the helpful concept of deposits and withdrawals in relationships. He talks about how, when good and kind things are done in a relationship, "deposits" are made in that person's "Love Bank" account. When hurtful or potentially threatening things happen, "withdrawals" are made.

Taking time to pour affection on your daughter will not only bring her a great deal of joy, but it will also pave the way for you to help build and shape her character. She'll give you permission to be tough (withdrawals) when she knows you've been tender (deposits).

The next chapter deals with correction and discipline. However, if you haven't made plenty of physical and verbal affection deposits in your account at your daughter's Love Bank, you'll overdraw. Your discipline check will bounce.

Insufficient funds.

Don't Forget to Love Her Mother

In late October 1974, our second daughter was born. We had been told that the second birth is always easier than the first. Be careful of people who tell you such things; they may lie about other things as well.

When our first daughter was born, we—mostly Bobbie—spent more than 14 hours in labor. But when Julie was born, it took almost 18 hours. The reason was that instead of being born headfirst the way most babies are born, she was in the breech position—feet first. The doctor told us that he may have been able to turn her body earlier, but because it was too late in her development to do this, Julie would be born breech. I had gone through all the predelivery classes, earning me a ticket to the delivery room. But because of the complications, when Bobbie was wheeled in, I had to wait in the hallway outside.

In about an hour, the doctor emerged from the operating room with two messages: "You have a little girl" and "There's something wrong with her leg."

The first time I held her, I could clearly see that her right leg hung limp. Although we've never gotten a conclusive diagnosis on Julie's leg, in those first few years of her life, we met with dozens of specialists and made many trips to hospitals all around the Chicago area. The trauma on us as a young couple was unbelievable. The professional warnings that Julie might never walk were difficult to handle, especially for her dad.[5]

Then, right in the middle of all this, I got a card from a close friend, several years my senior. After a few encouraging sentences, he wrote something I'll never forget. My wise friend said, "Don't forget that the most important thing you can do to be the dad Julie is going to need is to never stop loving her mother."

The words hit me like a straight left. Somehow, in the middle of all this uncertainty and pain, I had forgotten to keep my love for Bobbie on the front burner. The activity and stress that swirled around our baby girl had stolen some of my primary attention on my wife. His counsel was exactly what I needed, and I will always be grateful for the gift of those words.

And to you I pass on the same wisdom. As you learn how to demonstrate love to your daughter, don't forget that loving her mother is even more important. Through your open affection for your wife, your daughter will catch a firsthand glimpse of what it's like to be in a loving relationship with a man. It will help to guide her as she looks for the man who will someday be her husband. It will provide a model that she'll want to duplicate . . . because she will know exactly what it looks like.

Demonstrate affection to your daughter. And don't forget to keep loving your wife. In the eyes of your daughter, your affection toward her mother will be translated as affection toward her.

Builder's Checklist

1. *Touch your daughter.* This can be done in small, nondramatic ways—patting her knee as you drive to the store or squeezing her hand during church. Remember that touching your daughter has no age limitations.

2. *Speak affection to your daughter.* Take the time necessary to clearly speak words of affection to your girl. Don't be tempted into thinking you're doing something helpful if you do this on the run.

3. *Recognize that doing generous things is good, but it's not the same as genuine affection.* Because some dads may feel awkward with the idea of physical and verbal affection, they may rationalize, "Well, I'll just be extra generous at birthdays and Christmas." That's nice, but that's not going to do the job.

4. *Make plenty of deposits.* Your demonstrations of affection to your daughter will make deposits into her Love Bank account. No one is ever concerned about receiving too many deposits.

5. *Love your wife more.* The security that your daughter will feel when she sees how well you love her mother is incalculable. Affection you pour onto your wife in your daughter's presence gives her a sense of security. She may not be able to put this into words until she's a grown-up, but it's true.

Discipline

A Sledgehammer, a Couple of Crowbars, and a Level

> *If all our wishes were gratified, most of
> our pleasures would be destroyed.*
> —Richard Whately

We were in a hurry. I hollered upstairs to tell Bobbie that I'd go ahead and pull the car out of the garage. "I'll meet you on the driveway in front of the house," I said.

I didn't wait for her answer.

I crawled into our three-year-old Cutlass, more than a little anxious to get on with it. But when I turned the ignition key, I heard a weird sound. Over the years, with college cars and all, I've tried to start cars with dead batteries, but this particular noise had escaped me. The best way to describe it was that it was almost human sounding . . . like a guy with a kidney stone.[1]

In any case, my Oldsmobile was dead. I slid the gearshift to *N* and walked around to the front to push the car out of the garage. *Aaarrgghhh.* Kidney stones can be very heavy. Fortunately, our driveway sloped down to the street. Once the car had some momentum, I jumped behind the wheel to make sure the position of our mailbox did not get readjusted unintentionally.

After the car was all the way to the street, I walked back to the garage and fired up Julie's car. I backed it down the driveway and parked it face-to-face with my dead Olds. On my way back to the garage to get my jumper cables, a thought flashed across my mind: *Does Julie know what to do with jumper cables?* As a home-for-the-summer sophomore in college and with a little car of her own, she probably had never needed to jump-start a dead car.

Throughout their process of fathering, dads look for teachable moments. This was such a moment.

In a few minutes, 20-year-old Julie was standing on the street with me. I had the cables in my hands and was explaining that the black clamp goes on the negative battery post, while the red goes on the positive. I also observed that battery manufacturers now color-code battery posts—positive is red and negative is black.

As I stood there explaining how to safely take the charge from the good battery and use it to start the dead car, Julie interrupted me with a question. "Dad," she queried, "do you know *why* a battery has a positive and a negative?"

I took a long, deep breath, preparing my answer. (I also wasn't sure if this was a real question or if I was being set up by my science-and-math-loving daughter.)

I took another breath.

"They have a positive and a negative because in order to make anything work right, you *need* both a positive and a negative," I finally said, thinking a little enthusiasm might lead her to believe this was an actual answer.

Julie smiled at me, knowing I had just tried to bluff her and wasn't getting away with it. I smiled back, realizing that with two years of physics behind her, she knew full well why a battery has a positive and a negative. I used to know, but I forgot. She dropped the subject.

I went on with the jumper-cable lesson.

Regardless, the principle is correct. To make things work, there must be a positive and a negative. Both are necessary.

In the last chapter, we talked a lot about the positive—touching, squeezing, hugging, writing, and speaking tender words. As a dad, you must do those things. But if you had stopped reading at the end of that chapter and skipped this one, you'd be in deep weeds. Better said, your *daughter* would be in trouble.

There must be a positive side and a negative side to your relationship with her.

How much positive and how much negative? Please hear me on this: *100 percent* positive and *100 percent* negative. Crank them both up the whole way. Be the most affirming and tender dad you've ever heard

> *Be the most affirming and tender dad you've ever heard of, and be the most no-nonsense, strict father on the planet.*

of, *and* be the most no-nonsense, strict father on the planet. Under any conditions, please do not try to be one without the other. Learn to be good at both.

Using the Right Tools

When I'm about to frame a room with two-by-fours, two-by-sixes, and such, I always have three tools close by: a 16-pound sledgehammer, a Wonder Bar (this looks like a flat crowbar), and a four-foot level.

My job is to make sure every wall is perfectly vertical—the bubble on the level is *squarely* in the middle on every one. Why? Because I also enjoy hanging wallpaper, and if the internal structure of the walls isn't right, wallpapering—especially with striped wallpaper—is no fun at all.

Unfortunately, the sledgehammer and the crowbar are noisy to use. And though I prefer listening to jazz piano music to hearing the loud noises these tools make, I'm willing to endure that temporary discomfort in exchange for walls that are straight and true.

DISCIPLINE—THE NOUN AND THE VERB

The word *discipline* can be either a noun or a verb, depending on how it's used. The goal is to build a daughter who's a self-controlled person—a woman who is able to rein herself in; a woman whose interior structure is straight and true; a woman who possesses personal discipline. That's *discipline* the noun. It's what you're shooting for.

And how do you get there? *Discipline* the verb. An athlete achieves discipline (the noun) by submitting herself to being disciplined (the verb) by her coach or trainer . . . or dad. The joy and pleasure—positive—of being a disciplined person—noun—makes the pain—negative—of disciplining—verb—a worthwhile investment. Whew!

LOTS OF RAW MATERIAL

When your daughter is born, she has no discipline. None. If she's hungry, she cries. If she has to go, she goes. When all these things are taken care of and she still wants to make your life miserable, she may still feel like crying, so she does. When she's sleepy, she sleeps. And when she wakes up again and wants any of the above, she'll cry again. She has no ability to harness herself.

You, on the other hand, have discipline. Most of the time, you understand self-talk and restraint. You may feel like going absolutely berserk at some guy on the freeway who almost sideswipes you because he's text messaging, but you . . . er . . . uh . . . bad example. Anyway, for the most part, you live a disciplined life.

You may not feel like getting out of bed for work, but you do it anyway. You may not actually enjoy exercise, keeping your garage in order, using deodorant every day, or saying "Good morning" to the office receptionist, but you've learned to do those things. And they've become good habits. On a self-discipline scale of one to ten, let's say you're a seven. Or an eight.

Your brand-new daughter is a zero. No willpower at all. Your job with your little zero is to get her to a seven or eight, where you are, or higher if you've married well. How do you do this? Through *discipline*, the verb: setting guidelines and inspecting results. How long do you do this? Until her discipline—noun—kicks into autopilot.

In our culture, disciplining children is a controversial issue. Spanking is called "hitting." Verbal correction is referred to as "emotional abuse." In fact, this chapter may get me in a lot of trouble, but I'm willing to deal with it head-on.

Warning: The next several pages must be read by a disciplined person. In the wrong hands, this information will be like dynamite—explosive and very dangerous. In the right hands, it will be like a spark plug to gasoline vapor—explosive but accelerating your daughter forward.

Guidelines for Disciplining

To be a successful disciplinarian, you need to follow four extremely important guidelines. Remember that you don't discipline because you enjoy it. In fact, if doing it gives you pleasure, stop and get yourself some help.

The reason you discipline is that you're making an investment in your daughter. You're exercising your own discipline—consistently doing the right thing even if you don't feel like it—in creating discipline in your daughter. And remember that you are disciplining your daughter so that good behavior is the outflow of her heart, not to keep her from embarrassing you.

Rules must be clearly defined and consistently enforced

How would you like to play baseball if only the umpires knew where the foul lines were? And what if the lines changed from inning to inning? You'd be circling the bases, thinking you just hit a home run, but the umpire might tell you that in the *third* inning it would have been a round-tripper, but this is the *sixth* inning, and now it's an automatic out.

You'd trudge into the dugout and plop down on the bench, disliking the umpire and probably the whole stupid game as well. Who would blame you?

Set guidelines for your young daughter: Toys back in the box when she's done playing; finish her vegetables before enjoying dessert; reasonable limits on electronics or text messaging; in bed by nine o'clock; no disrespectful back talking allowed; and so on. Be sure she clearly understands. Don't make these rules up as you go. If you do, no punishment should be given on the first infraction.

Then be consistent with the rules and the penalties when rules are deliberately broken. Never, ever punish for youthful forgetfulness, clumsiness, and honest mistakes.

Discipline must be swift

The effectiveness of your discipline will often depend on the amount of time between the infraction and the corresponding correction—the less time the more effective; the more time the less effective.

Several years ago, a fad swept the country. It encouraged parents to count to three prior to expecting their child to obey. I can envision these parents in the grocery store. Their young son is walking toward a man-sized pyramid of canned green beans on special. He's got total annihilation of the display in mind, and his mother tells him, "You come back here right now, Sheldon."

Sheldon pauses, glancing over his right shoulder to see if the voice is his mother's and, if it is, whether she's actually addressing him. Nice try, Sheldon.

He turns back toward Del Monte Mountain, accelerating his pace.

"Sheldon, I said you come back here," pleads his mother. Then, almost robotically, she begins to count: "One, two-o-o . . ."

Watching this bizarre scene, I'm taken back to all-neighborhood, all-evening Kick the Can marathons. I can see the kid who's "it" standing with his face against the coarse bark of the huge elm tree in our front yard and counting, his hands cupped around the outside of his eyes. The mother in the grocery store reminds me of one of those youngsters counting—neither one of them is seeing very clearly.

Don't count.

The guideline for your daughter is this: When your dad—or your mother—asks you to obey, you obey. When do you obey? The first time you're asked.

Our girls knew about this so well that when they hesitated, we would say, "When do you obey?" And they would respond, "The first time." ("The foost tahm" before they could enunciate well.)

You're going to find this guideline extremely inconvenient. Why? Because you and I are, by nature, lazy. We would rather delay the consequence of our daughter's misbehavior until a more convenient moment: "Go to your room until this football game reaches halftime, *then* we'll deal with your lack of self-control."

Discipline must be painful

Come with me, right now, on a little mental journey to your favorite state penitentiary. We're going to walk up and down the cell blocks conducting brief interviews with the various inmates. We're going to ask them if this is what they had in mind when they were kids. We'll ask them if they're happy. Fulfilled. Living the life they had dreamed about.

Or are they in pain?

There may be nothing as awful—or painful—as living an undisciplined life and not being able to go back and fix it. People waste their lives, sitting in a 9-by-12 in Leavenworth, Kansas, having acted spontaneously. For one moment in time, they did what came naturally, and now they're sitting out their life.

In his classic, best-selling book *The Road Less Traveled*, M. Scott Peck called life "hard." He was right. And an undisciplined life is even harder and more painful.

Just below my left shoulder, at the top of my arm, is a dime-sized scar. A doctor gave me that scar when I was seven. All I remember about getting my smallpox vaccination was that he used two needles to inflict this terrible thing on me.

In the past few years, I've learned what a smallpox vaccination really is. It's literally . . . smallpox. Of course, it's administered safely, under sound medical conditions, but it's actually smallpox—a little dose of *the real thing*.

Now, please follow me on this one: If living out an undisciplined life is an extremely unpleasant and painful experience, then disciplining a person toward self-discipline should mean small doses of the real thing—painful inflictions under sound and loving family conditions.

And what constitutes "painful" discipline?

For starters, it's *not* words.

Imagine that you are speeding along a lonesome country road, oblivious to the speed limit. Suddenly, in the distance, you see a person—he looks a lot like a police officer—standing on the shoulder. After you fly past him, you see him in your rearview mirror, screaming at you. Of course, traveling at Mach 1, you can't actually hear anything. But you can tell he's really into it, because he's jumping up and down and shaking his fists.

Do you slow down? Not unless you've inadvertently eased up on the accelerator while watching the officer dance.

Unfortunately—and this is from personal experience—that's not what really happens. Police officers understand the value of swift (do not try to outrun that benign-looking car) and painful (what else could you have done with that $250?) action as a direct result of your intentional (you saw the signs) disobedience.

For your daughter, painful discipline may be a spanking. Our granddaughter Harper was itching to disobey her mom and crawl out of her bed when she was told to lie down because it was bedtime. "Harper," her mother said sternly, "what happens when we disobey our daddy?"

"Daddy pank me," Harper responded, obediently lying down. She may have been able to endure a lecture or the threat of a suspended privilege the next day, but a spanking right now was something to be avoided. After all, who wants to be "panked"? Harper weighed her options, and obeying won the day.

Or a punishment may be a moratorium from something your daughter really enjoys; her iPod Touch or something else electronic comes to mind. But for it to be effective, it must provide enough discomfort that she says to herself, *You know, that wasn't fun. I think I'll do whatever I can to avoid that in the future.*

Mission accomplished.

Discipline must be fair

The Old Testament calls it "an eye for an eye and a tooth for a tooth" (Exodus 21:24). And, until recently, I had no idea what that really meant.

Actually, it's a simple principle: Jewish law provided that if you stole a man's mule, you had to replace it. If you burned down a man's barn, you were responsible for rebuilding it. If you took someone's life, you should pay with your own.

Fairness in disciplining means that the punishment should match the "crime." If your daughter leaves a mess, make her clean it up. Don't spank her for this. If she hurts her friend, walk her to her friend's house and make her ask for forgiveness. Don't spank her for this. If she blatantly disobeys you or speaks disrespectfully to you, it's probably time for something more painful. Something with consequences.

Remember that you're giving her a little dose of the real thing.

A spanking—or another effective form of punishment that you and your wife have settled on—when she's six is *not as painful* as a lost job or a broken marriage when she's 28 because you didn't teach her how to control her tongue. She might not understand this when she's six, but swift, painful, and fair punishment is one of the most important "gifts" you'll ever give your daughter.

Time Out for Some Perspective

You can be sure that some folks will read *swift* and *painful* and say this book advocates hauling off and blasting your daughter the moment she steps out of line. *No, no, no.* I'm not advocating that. That kind of rash punishment is despicable. It's often filled with rage, and the one being disciplined usually walks away more angry at the one who delivered the correction than she is at herself for the infraction.

Mission *not* accomplished.

Take a moment when your daughter has disobeyed—or whatever—to calm down. Then talk to her about what she did and why you believe it deserves punishment.

Take a deep breath. You're teaching her something; you're not looking for a chance to blow off steam. You're not getting even.

Along those lines, here are a few hints:

1. No yelling. Yes, when your daughter has disobeyed, your voice is going to be more intense than when you're asking your server for more coffee, but no yelling allowed. Angry outbursts are *never* productive. Yelling makes you look and sound silly and does not motivate your child. It will most often direct itself to you or, worse, to your daughter's *person* rather than to her *deed.* Flag on the play. If you yell at your daughter, you *must* apologize to her, which doesn't do much for the lesson *she's* supposed to be learning.

2. Spank under control. My wife and I spanked our girls by holding them over our knee and paddling about 15 times with our hand. Your hand will be an adequate pain gauge, helping you not to forget that some serious discomfort is going on here. We didn't spank hard. It was the repetition that communicated the message. This was not an angry swat; this was a spanking. There's a big difference. If you hit your daughter in anger, you *must* apologize to her, which doesn't do much for the lesson *she's* supposed to be learning.

Some experts recommend using a neutral object—a ruler, a wooden spoon, or a hair brush—for spanking. In their professional opinion, this object represents a more distant instrument than a parent's hand—something that should be reserved for holding and loving your child. But our experience was that our hand, like the car battery with positive and negative poles, was the proper instrument for both— that physical punishment was as intentional and personal as physical tenderness.

Spanking was not something we did *to* our daughters. We did this *for* our daughters. It was a shared and painful experience, acknowledging that there had been a breach in our relationship that must be bridged. Like a grain of sand in your eye, it's a "foreign object" that must be excised. It wasn't a happy moment in our relationship, but ultimately, it became a building block, as important between us as our occasional visits to the frozen-yogurt shop.

> *If you embarrass your daughter, shame on you.*

3. *Always punish privately.* If you embarrass your daughter, shame on *you*. Like yelling, creating embarrassment focuses pain on the wrong thing. If you're in public and she has just done something punishable, try to catch her eye. Let her know you saw what she did, and you're not pleased. She'll get the message. You may have to take her to another room to punish her, but do your best to avoid a public place that creates an unnecessary, embarrassing event.

Disciplining your daughter is a private thing. It cannot be a display. If you are in public, create a small space where you have her undivided attention. You may need to squat down and take her face in your hands and create a bubble for just the two of you.

Don't let your daughter catch you telling your friends—or, worse, *her* friends—about it, either. If you embarrass your daughter, you *must* apologize to her, which doesn't do much for the lesson *she's* supposed to be learning.

SOMETHING MAGIC INSIDE?

In 2001, a brand-new transportation product was unveiled that some thought would radically change the way people transported themselves, particularly in crowded, big-city downtowns.

Dean Kamen, the inventor who created the Segway, hoped that this electric two-wheeler would literally replace the automobile in places that were gridlocked with snarling traffic. But, Americans are addicted to their cars, and this transformation did not happen.

Anyway, you have seen Segways. Maybe you've had the fun of riding one and know that you can command it simply by shifting your body weight. You lean forward and it goes forward. You lean back and it goes in reverse.

But even though it didn't completely reinvent transformation, the Segway has grown into a very useful mode of transportation for security people and law enforcement officers, especially in large areas like airports and shopping malls.

The magic of the Segway is an assembly of gyroscopes mounted inside the footpad. These devices have been simply described as spinning wheels inside stable frames that are programmed to go a certain direction. Because of these gyroscopes, Segways have an almost perfect safety record. Unless their rider is using them improperly, a Segway cannot fall down. They have, as my mother used to say, "a mind of their own."

Gyroscopes are also used in airplanes and race cars to keep them on course.

You know where this is taking us, don't you?

Discipline planted deep inside your daughter will act like a gyroscope. From the time she is very young, you are helping her build her own gyroscope. Regardless of external influences and pressure, she will be able to hold a steady course because of what's inside. This is an amazing and wonderful thing to see.

SAY NO ONCE A DAY

This may sound a bit quirky, but when our girls were young, we experimented with self-discipline. We created a playful exchange called the "No Game." We challenged everyone around the supper table to "say no to yourself at least one time tomorrow, and then report your story tomorrow night at dinner."

It didn't have to be a bad thing we were saying no to, just something like turning the television off a half hour before we really wanted to or limiting our after-school snack to one cookie instead of two. This was decades before the advent of handheld electronics. Today the opportunities for a good "no" are manifold.

At dinnertime the following evening, we talked about how well we did. We made it fun, but this game gave all of us the ability to keep ourselves in check. Discipline, the noun.

Reports the next day were things like the following:

Dad's report: "At lunch today, I was about to order a slice of pie for dessert, but I decided that since I had dessert yesterday, I'd say no today. So I said no."

Everyone cheered Dad's good report, not necessarily because he was getting a little round and needed to go on a diet, but because he was able to tell himself no and make it stick.

Teenage daughter's report: "I was talking with my best friend on my phone. I had some homework that needed to be finished, so I told her I could talk for only five more minutes. In a little while, I glanced back at the clock and realized my time was up. Even though I *really* wanted to keep talking, I told my friend that I had work to do and ended the call."

The whole family celebrated, not because she didn't have enough minutes on her phone package, but because our daughter made a rule and then obeyed it, all on her own.

Little girl's report: "My friend offered me some leftover Halloween candy right before dinner, and I said, 'No, thank you.'"

Again, the family cheered our daughter's ability to make a good decision all by herself.

We were learning together, before being faced with life-and-death situations, to fine-tune our own self-imposed navigation systems.

Your job, as the father of a girl, is to use externally imposed discipline through punishments or even through playing the "No Game," and to create the internal discipline—the gyroscope—that gives her a will of her own.

The things in your daughter's world that are not necessarily bad but still need to be controlled—balanced or aligned properly—will be the toughest disciplining challenge for you as her dad. For example, eating is a good idea. Three solid meals a day keeps your girl healthy and strong. But overeating or being hooked on foods that provide no nutrition is not good. Instead of the "No Game," you will be playing the "No More Game."

As you and I discussed earlier, electronics are good. But too much electronics—enough to get in the way of family time, undistracted communication, or safe driving—is not good. Again, the "No More Game."

Sooner than you can imagine, the day will arrive when your daughter will make every decision—big and small—without your direct influence. What you want is for her to make good choices simply because they're good choices—internal gyroscopes headed in the right direction—not because her dad will be there to make sure they're good choices!

GOD'S IDEA OF A GOOD TIME

At the very moment I'm writing this, I'm looking out on a mid-September Central Florida morning. The sky is crystal clear, the bluest blue you could ever imagine. Because we've had lots of rain, our yard is a spectacular shade of green. Because it's early in the day, the palm trees in front of our house are standing beautiful, motionless, and strong.[2]

But as hard as it may be for me to imagine, the Garden of Eden makes the scene out my window look like a smoldering city dump.

Not only was Eden pretty to look at, but it was also perfect in every way. Man's relationship to woman was flawless. Woman's relationship to man was without dissension or fear. And both of their relationships with their Creator were impeccable. Adam and Eve delighted in all of this.

Amazingly, right in the middle of this pristine flawlessness was a "no"—an exquisite tree whose fruit couldn't be eaten. Isn't that amazing? The Garden of Eden included a no.

Most of the time, I think of enjoyment as meaning no boundaries. No inhibitions. No noes, if you will. All yeses. But like the battery in my dead Oldsmobile, in order to work properly, life must include the positive *and* the negative.

RALPH FOOTE

When I was a senior in college, I was pushing the edges a little on conduct. I guess my parents' teaching and admonitions were somewhere between planting and harvesting in my heart, if you know what I mean.

Because of that, I often stayed out late. I don't mean just late, I mean *late*. And sometimes, in returning to campus, I'd see the darkened image of a person running along the country roads that surrounded our school. Here it was, the middle of the night, and this guy was running all by himself.

I found out that the runner was a sophomore from a small Indiana town. His name was Ralph Foote, and he was a serious runner. I'm not exactly sure how often I saw Ralph on his midnight runs; I only know that it was many, many times.

I remember thinking, *Poor Ralph. College life certainly isn't as much fun for him as it is for me. Why doesn't he stop all this running and begin to enjoy himself?*

The following spring, I learned that the track coach was looking for some help for the conference track meet. Taylor University was hosting the event, and there was a call for timers and helpers to move hurdles, rake the sand in the broad-jump pit, set the bars for the high jump and pole vault, and so forth. I volunteered.

Near the end of the afternoon at the track meet, the announcer called the runners to the starting line for the two-mile run. Having been a wannabe distance runner in junior high, I had always been impressed by those who had the guts to run the long ones. And since I didn't have any current assignments for other events, I crawled up to the top of the press tower to watch.

When the gun sounded, the mass of runners took off like a single, multiheaded creature. But by the end of the second lap, the creature had substantially thinned out. Several men—maybe six or seven—were leading; the rest of the field stretched out for 30 yards.

By the time the runners finished four laps—the first mile—the distance between the guys in front and those in the back was the length of the straightaway—almost a full half lap. The lead pack was down to three.

This running triplet hung together for three more laps. Step for step, they were pacing each other with gliding, synchronized strides.

As the timers in the press box glanced at their watches, the excitement began to build. "There could be a new conference record set in the two-mile," I overheard them say. Maybe a new *state* record.

In distance races, the starter fires the gun when the first runner begins his last lap. This is cleverly referred to as the "gun lap." When the gun sounded, announcing that this running triumvirate had crossed the starting line for the last time, something unbelievable happened. As I write these words, over 45 years later, I feel the overwhelming emotion of what I saw that day as though I'm experiencing it for the first time.

Before the sound of the shot had finished reverberating through the woods behind the track, a single runner seemed to explode from the pack of three. As though propelled by a slingshot, he took off in a dead sprint. And although the other two runners had picked up their own paces a bit, it looked as though they had come to a complete stop.

The entire stadium came to its feet. Field-event competitors finishing their efforts stood frozen. The lead runner, a sophomore named Ralph Foote, had been waiting for this moment. The faithful discipline of late-night running on those lonely Indiana country roads was seeking its rightful reward.

For a full quarter mile, Ralph did not slow his pace. The dead sprint he began at the start of the gun lap did not slack.

By the time Ralph rounded the last turn for the final dash to the tape, every person in the stadium was screaming for this 19-year-old. Even the athletes and coaches from other schools were cheering him on.

When the time was posted, Ralph Foote had scraped a full 11 seconds off the school record in the two-mile, and more than 10 seconds off the conference record. (The spring before, he had broken the previous conference record by 19.3 seconds! And just for good measure, Ralph set still another new record—this time the state mark—in the two-mile one year later.)

I have a question: Who was the happiest man in the stadium that Saturday afternoon?

Correct. It was Ralph Foote.

Why? Because he had turned the disciplining and grueling pain of relentless, no-pizza-with-his-buddies, late-night training into the reward of being the most disciplined two-miler in the history of the school. And the conference. And the state.

Discipline is its *own* reward.

Your assignment is to brand an image of your daughter as a happy, balanced, disciplined, and complete woman in your mind. Then create a system of swift, painful, and fair discipline that successfully gets her to that destination.

Your job is not to be *liked*. Your job is to love her by being *faithful* and *effective*. If you're doing the right things, there will be days when you'll come in dead last in the Dad of the Year Sweepstakes. That's okay. Don't give up. Hang in there. This one's especially tough for quitters like us. But you can do it.

Does this sound like a lot of gut-wrenching work? Well, there *are* days when it's not that easy, but the whole process can be a lot of fun, too. We're going to talk about that next.

Builder's Checklist

1. *Remember that the "good life" is both positive and negative.* Although we tend to believe that positive is always good and negative is always bad, everything truly worthwhile includes both.

2. *Think of discipline as both a verb and a noun.* To help your daughter reach the goal of internal self-discipline (the noun), it's necessary to discipline (the verb) her externally.

3. *Make punishment swift, painful, and fair.* Waiting too long between the infraction and the penalty diminishes the impact of the punishment. A consequence that isn't painful is not a consequence at all; it's simply a slight inconvenience. On the

other hand, when the sentence outmatches the severity of the crime, it will be seen as unfair and will lose its impact.

4. *Be sure your life matches your words.* To be the disciplinarian your daughter needs, your life and habits need to match your words.

5. *Teach that discipline is its own reward.* The achievement of personal discipline can be a great thrill all by itself. You don't have to be a distance runner breaking records for this to have significant value.

LAUGHTER

Did You Hear the One About . . . ?

*Laughter is the shortest distance
between two people.*
—VICTOR BORGE

In March 1982, I received a letter that changed my life. At least, that's what it said it was going to do.

The outside of the envelope promised that "You have already won." The letter inside explained the details. My name had been "specially drawn" from a list of millions, and of the eight wonderful awards listed, I had won one of the prizes with a check mark next to it. Here was the checked list:

A Jeep Cherokee	I love Jeeps. I always wanted one.
A boat	Waterskiing is one of my favorite sports.
A Weed Eater	That's probably the one I really won, because it's the cheapest. But hey, my lawn could use a Weed Eater.
A huge flat-screen TV	Now you're talking—Chicago Bears—life-sized!

All we had to do to claim our prize was drive to Fort Worth—about 100 miles away—and listen to a "brief, two-hour presentation." Although the girls were skeptical, I was able to talk them into making the trip with some subtle salesmanship:

"If we win the television, I'll let you stay up every night as long as you want for the rest of your life. You can watch any show, and I'll never tell you to turn it off."

"If we win the Jeep, I'll let you drive. So what if you're only 11 and 8! Silly rules like having a driver's license aren't really necessary. Plus, I have some lawyer friends."

"If we win the Weed Eater, I'll cut your grass when you get married and have a house of your own."

"If we win the boat . . ."

As I said, they agreed to take the trip to Fort Worth.

When we arrived at Lake Awesome and Spectacular Estates and Country Club, I remember being impressed with the massive brick-and-stone entrance. It was the size of Wrigley Field, complete with more meticulous landscaping than the entrance to Busch Gardens. Unfortunately, that's all there was. No permanent buildings. No golf course. Come to think of it, no lake, either. Just the huge entrance nicely paved and curbed, with underground utilities, and roads leading to more nicely paved roads with curbs.

There were also several double-wide trailers just inside the entrance, where we had the rare opportunity of meeting Nick, our friendly and talkative salesman. My guess was that Nick had been given the choice of two years down the river, 200 hours of community service, or this.

As he got deeper and deeper into his presentation, I could see that I was losing my family. Whenever I caught their eyes, they'd give me this "Please, please, get me out of here or I'll die" look. So I quickly fixed that problem.

I stopped looking at them.

Exactly two hours later, Nick was finished—more finished than he ever knew. He asked if we were interested in purchasing a lot at Lake Awesome and Spectacular, and after I spent enough time appearing to seriously think about it, I told him I thought we'd need to put that decision on hold. *Yeah, like on hold till the glaciers make it to Fort Worth.*

Then, acting very disappointed at our decision to pass on this once-in-a-lifetime opportunity, he asked to see our letter, the one promising the prize. I gladly handed it over. As he scanned the list of "awards we had won," I looked at my family with that air of confident assurance. I was thinking, *This'll be worth it all, girls. In just a few moments, you'll forget the past two hours of torture. You'll be happy, and I'll be a hero.*

After the charade of checking the code number on our letter against the master notebook of code numbers, Nick stroked his chin, gave a little *hmmm* sound, and raised his eyebrows to indicate he really regretted having to part with such a valuable thing. "It looks like you've won the boat," he finally announced.

The girls squealed with delight. "A boat! Wow, Dad, a boat!"

Oh no, I remember thinking, *I don't have a trailer hitch on my car.* This is the truth. That thought *really* crossed my mind.

Nick excused himself to go get the boat, and we walked outside to the front of the double-wide, where my hitchless car was parked. The girls asked if I thought we might be able to put the boat into a lake near our home. I assured them we'd do that just as soon as possible.

In a few minutes, Nick appeared with the boat . . . in his hand. It was the inflate-to-25-pounds, made-in-the-proud-and-sovereign-Republic-of-Barbados Sea Cloud Sport Boat. "*Warning: Not to be used as a life preserver*" was printed on the side of the clear plastic bag he proudly handed me.

The girls gasped, but before they could actually say anything, I had them corralled into the car, and we were off, driving back through—for the last time ever—the massive brick-and-stone entrance.

Good-bye, Lake Whatever and Who Cares Estates.

The drive back to our home was not pleasant. I apologized for being so stupid and gullible. I apologized again. I promised that when I died, all my estate would be split between the two girls, and that even if we had more kids, because they hadn't been forced to endure Nick, the new ones wouldn't get a dime.

We stopped for sundaes.

BE HAPPY

The story of the Sea Cloud Sport Boat has provided our family with more value than any 16-foot, fiberglass sloop ever could have. I've told the story countless times. The girls have brought friends home and said, "Dad, tell Audrey the story of the Sea Cloud Sport Boat." And we've laughed again.

In the Gospels, Jesus opened the Sermon on the Mount—His magnum opus sermon—with a description of what it takes to be happy. It's almost as though He were saying, "You'll know you've arrived in My kingdom when your life is marked with happiness."

BE FUN TO LIVE WITH

> *Laugh with your girl. Be silly. Fill your home with joy. Buy a pair of Groucho Marx glasses and come to dinner wearing them.*

Laugh with your girl. Be goofy in public. Be silly at home. Fill your family with joy. Buy a pair of Groucho Marx glasses and come to dinner wearing them.[1] Walk into the room with your arms outstretched, your hands in the clawed position, growling like a grizzly bear, and "attack" your girl, tousling her hair and tickling her. Do be careful, because you're much bigger and stronger. However, if your wife isn't saying, "Honey, be careful," you're not doing it right! You're not acting "grizzly" enough.

When I had one of my daughters on the floor, I'd nuzzle my face into the soft skin of her neck and blow out, making a loud "*ZZZ-rrrrbbbttl.*" She would squeal. Her mother would call from the other room, "Hey, what are you doing in there?"

"Nothing," I'd reply innocently.

We'd look at each other and giggle knowingly.

PRETTY FUNNY STUFF

Go to a bookstore and buy a riddle book. Okay, so they're a little corny, but your girl will love them. Here are a few examples. Remember that these are for you to use with your daughter, so there's no need to smile yourself.

Which side of a chicken has the most feathers? The outside.

Where do sheep get their hair cut? At the baa-baa shop.

Why don't ducks tell jokes when they're flying? They might quack up.

Why are fish so smart? Because they live in schools.

How do baby birds learn to fly? They wing it.

Why do bees hum? Because they don't know the words.

What did the beaver say to the tree? It's been nice gnawing you.

Buy other fun books. One of our favorites was *Hand, Hand, Fingers, Thumb.* I would read the book to the girls and act it out while I was reading: "Millions of fingers, millions of thumbs, millions of monkeys drumming on drums, Dum ditty dum ditty dum dum dum." When we'd get to that last part, one of the girls would "read" along, "Dum ditty dum ditty dum dum dum."

We would laugh.

When the girls got a little older, we bought a video copy of the classic comedy *What's Up, Doc?* with Ryan O'Neal and Barbra Streisand. We watched the video so many times that we—especially the girls—

had nearly every line memorized. Then there were times when lines like "Don't shoot me, I'm part Italian" or "Eunice, there's a person named Eunice?" would fit with something we were talking about.

And we would laugh.

You will have your own silly family movie with lines you'll repeat and laugh about. *Napoleon Dynamite* and *Little Rascals* are favorites for our grandkids and their parents. Pick-up lines from movies like these can become humor shorthand—inside-the-family humor—for the rest of their lives.

"Do the chickens have large talons?"

"Quick, what's the number for 9-1-1?"

SLUG BUG

Someone gave our grandson Luke the idea to sock me when he'd see a VW Bug. The first time this happened, we were walking across the Chick-fil-A parking lot on our way to waffle fries. "Look, Granddaddy," Luke called out, "Slug Bug." And with that he wheeled around and let me have it. Girls may not appreciate a hitting game as much as boys, but you can improvise. Make every experience with your daughter an opportunity for fun.

One of our granddaughters' favorites was "This little piggy went to market; this little piggy stayed home; this little piggy had roast beef; this little piggy had none; and this little piggy cried 'wee wee wee' all the way home." Okay, this may have been popular before your time, but try it when your daughter is barefooted. Each of the piggies is one of her toes that you take in your fingers and wiggle, starting with the big one and ending with her baby toe. That's the one that cries "wee wee wee" all the way home. Somehow, when gifts were handed out, I received the ability to talk like Donald Duck. When I combine the piggy-toe thing with Donald Duck, it's a winner.

Rules for Laughter

Yes, there are rules even for laughter. Unless you follow several guidelines, even laughter could become an unfortunate and hurtful thing.

Laugh with your girl, never at her

"I was just kidding" rarely fixes a clumsy attempt at person-directed humor. Especially when your daughter is young, you must be careful about the kind of laughter you employ. If it's at your daughter's expense, you'll pay.

Remember that your daughter has a tender and easily broken heart. You must do your best to protect it.

Find things you can do together that are fun. I've already mentioned funny books and silly movies and grizzly bears, but you can add your own repertoire to that list, doing unpredictable and crazy things.

Choose spontaneity over nutrition

One Friday night, Charles—a serious-minded, CPA-type friend—announced to his daughter, Meg, that he was taking her to breakfast the next morning. She was delighted. Breakfast with Dad was always a lot of fun.

Early the next morning, Charles busied himself with chores around the house, telling his daughter that "in just a little while, we'll be leaving for breakfast." By ten o'clock, they were off.

"Where are we going for breakfast?" Meg wondered aloud.

"Oh, a special breakfast place" was all Charles would say.

In a few minutes, Charles brought his car to a stop in front of the local Ben & Jerry's. "We're here, Meg," he announced.

"Dad, this is an ice-cream place. We don't eat ice cream for breakfast," she said.

"*Today* we do," Charles responded.

In telling me the story, my friend recalled his delight in treating his six-year-old to a lavish banana fudge royal sundae: "Meg was completely shocked by my impulsive, out-of-character morning treat. For weeks she told everybody she saw that her daddy had bought her ice cream for breakfast." And Charles's face told me that the exchange of ice cream for something more nutritious was well worth it.

He also told me he'd had to talk his wife into this one before pulling it off.

Make your daughter laugh.

Laugh at circumstances

Every family has humorous experiences. Ours included the Sea Cloud Sport Boat and many others.

Gary Smalley tells stories of family camping trips. His reason for taking his family on those excursions was that every trip included a crisis: thunderstorms, raccoons, poison ivy . . . the possibilities are endless.

Even if your family isn't into inflatable "ski" boats or camping trips, there are plenty of things you can do together. These activities create the circumstances that naturally produce wonderful, laughable memories.

You can go bowling. You can take long hikes. You can put a jungle gym in your backyard or go to a city park where they have lots of things a dad can do with his daughter—swings, slides, and crawl-through things.

Hint: Always take pictures. Reach out with your cell phone and take a "selfie" with silly faces or ask other people if they would please take yours for you. As your daughter grows up, these photos of you together will become permanent reminders of those happy times you shared.

Play games

Christopher made hide-and-seek a regular homemade game. When he'd come home from work, one of his daughters would call from somewhere in the house, challenging him to "come find me." Your house doesn't have to be big for this game to be great fun.

Because he came from a home where table games were almost reverenced, Jon loves Rummikub, Apples to Apples, Ticket to Ride, and Sequence. In fact, it was Jon who introduced us to Toss Up, a color dice game that works with kids of all ages and can easily travel in your pocket. This one's our favorite.

Chutes and Ladders, slapjack, or doing puzzles together will give you hours of fun with your girl. Avoid the temptation to always play electronic games. Because they often move very fast, these games sometimes inhibit your ability to interact with each other, not to mention the fact that they were created in such a way that grown-ups always lose.

Not every game you play with your girl needs to be store-bought, either. For example, you can play the Toes and Fingers game. The first time we played it, we were on a family vacation. For some reason, we started comparing the relative length of our fingers. Each person held up his or her hand with the fingers right next to each other, taking-an-oath style. We discovered that my index finger is shorter than my ring finger, and my middle finger is the longest, but the pattern was different with each of us. Then we decided to check out our toes, so we took off our socks, lay on our backs next to each other, and held our feet aloft.

Guess what? Our toes were different too. I was the only one with a second toe longer than my big toe. Missy's little toe looked like a sprout on a potato you've left in the basement too long. I can still see us lying there comparing our toes, and it still makes me laugh.

On car trips, we made up all kinds of fun games. We would divide the car into two teams, the left side and the right side. Then we'd silently count cows, sheep, and horses. Cows were 1 point, sheep were 5 points, and horses were 10. Dogs, cats, and birds didn't count. You could count only the animals on your side. However, if you spotted a graveyard on your opponents' side, all their animals were "dead," and they would have to start over.

The Alphabet Game was also a favorite. Starting with "Ready, go," each person in the car would silently collect each of the letters of the alphabet from road signs. They had to be gathered in order—you'll find yourself praying for *j*'s and *q*'s—and no fair turning around to see signs on the other side of the road. That would have made it unfair for the driver. We made this rule because I'm such a competitor that I might have wrecked the car looking for a missing letter . . . like *p* for paramedic! The first person to find *z* would holler out the letter, and the game was over.

Sometimes on trips, we would "collect" license plates from as many states as possible.

Laugh at yourself

Both our girls were school cheerleaders. Occasionally they would coerce me into learning one of their favorite cheers. Even though I knew my level of coordination was no match for that of limber and graceful girls, I would still give it a try. Those sessions always ended with hilarious laughter directed at this clumsy, inflexible dad trying to put all the moves of the cheer together. Tough as some of those ego-busting adventures were, I tried to make sure I laughed too.

The girls always loved it when I told stories of my childhood. Sometimes on trips I would tell them some of the silly things I did as a little boy or teenager. For some reason, they loved to hear about the times I got in trouble. They'd laugh at my foolishness, and because a lot of years had passed since I did the stupid thing I was telling them about, I'd laugh too.

Several years ago, it dawned on me that life was getting too serious. I was deeply entrenched in the perils of keeping a small business afloat. All my working life, payroll day had been a happy day. But since I was now one of the owners, payroll was a treacherous day. The one day every two weeks when I should have had a happy face, I looked worse than usual. My family started to remind me that I was "looking too serious these days."

So, the next time I was in our local bookstore, I wandered over to the humor section. Riffling through the selection of books, I discovered some pretty funny stuff. I bought several titles. In reading those books and the many others I've bought since, I discovered that although I *wanted* to be fun (and funny), I just didn't have enough material. Those books were just what I needed.

I also bought *The Far Side* daily calendar and a few books of Gary Larson's collections. Describing one of his bizarre cartoons to my family can be as funny as reading it for the first time.

Every Dave Barry book published is in my library. Reading these and sometimes referring back to them puts me in a happy state of mind. I've read these on airplanes and noticed the folks sitting close by wonder why I'm buckled over laughing. They're jealous.

Reading such material brought something important to my conscious mind: There are lots of funny things about *me*. And the same will be true of you. I had never thought about that before. But visiting those humorists and seeing them laugh at themselves and at life as it really is gave me permission to uncover those things about myself that are, well, laughable.

YouTube can be another good place to find funny stuff, although you need to be careful with this and always be there with your daughter when you're looking at it. Our grandkids introduced me to Tim Hawkins, whose stand-up comedy is without equal. It's also clean. We have watched many of his clips and silly songs together.

In his wonderful and refreshing book *Laugh Again,* Charles Swindoll said it like this:

Far too many adults I know are serious as a heart attack. They live with their fists tightened, and they die with deep frowns. They cannot remember when they last took a chance or risked trying something new. The last time they tried something really wild they were nine years old. I ask you, where's the fun? Let's face it, you and I are getting older—it's high time we stop acting like it!

And as our daughters grow older themselves, my ability to enjoy growing older, to laugh at myself, gives them less fear about the same thing—getting older. Perhaps it even gives them the chance to find humor in their own shortcomings, foibles, and idiosyncrasies today.

Laugh with your daughter.

Builder's Checklist

1. *Retell the stories that last a lifetime.* There are situations we've gotten ourselves into that make great material for the rest of our lives. Don't forget to reminisce with your family about those fateful situations. It's great fun.

2. *Ask yourself, "Am I fun to live with?"* Several years ago, a friend said to me, "Every once in a while, I stop and think what it must be like to live with me." What a good thing to do.

3. *Remember the five rules for laughter:*
   - Laugh *with* your girl, never *at* her. Play "grizzly bear," buy riddle books, and rent silly videos.
   - Laugh at circumstances. Tell tales of your own growing up, or what happened on a camping trip.
   - Choose spontaneity over nutrition. Choose ice cream every now and again. Your daughter will laugh at being able to break the nutrition rules.
   - Play games, either store-bought or made-up. Occasionally avoid the easy default to movies or game systems on car trips and make up stuff that engages one another in conversation and laughter.
   - Laugh at yourself. Let your mistakes and foibles be the stuff of family humor. It'll be okay. You'll survive!

4. *Have fun with your daughter.* Turn off the electronic distractions. Get out a game and play it with your girl. There are plenty to choose from, regardless of her age . . . or yours.

FAITH

Jesus Loves Me, This I Know

> *The great door sighs, then opens, and a child*
> *enters the church and kneels at the front pew.*
> *The Maker of the Universe has smiled. He*
> *made the church for this one interview.*
> —DANIEL SARGENT

When our youngest granddaughter Ella was four, her parents took her and her older sister, Harper, to a water park. The North Carolina sun was toasty enough to keep everyone warm but not so hot that it felt like a live barbecue. It was a perfect day for playing outside. In the water.

The tallest slide stood tall and bold in the center, taunting even the bravest child—and her daddy—to challenge its certain danger. The velocity of the descending sliders combined with its twists and turns made it the crown jewel of the park. After a few hours of playing on the smaller slides and watching other children take their run on the big one, Ella made two decisions. First, she was ready for the experience. This looked too exciting to miss. And second, she would do it only if her daddy joined her.

So Christopher and Ella made their way up the stairs to the launch area where noisy children waited their turn. As they ascended the steps,

Ella hung onto her daddy's hand. "It felt like Ella's grip on my hand got tighter with each one," Christopher told me. Finally, the duet reached the top.

At the full height of the slide, tickles of panic swept Christopher's mind. *This thing is a lot higher than it looks from down below*, he thought to himself. But there would be no admitting his fear to his frightened daughter. And certainly no turning back.

After a few minutes, it was Christopher and Ella's turn. The young helper at the top—a psychology major at the local junior college, no doubt—greeted them. Stretching out his hand, he reached toward Ella.

"You're next, young lady. Do you want to go alone?" he asked.

Gripping her daddy's hand even tighter, Ella looked up at Christopher. Her eyes widened but she did not answer. She shook her head with undeniable resolve. Christopher leaned down, knowing that Ella wanted to tell him something in private.

"I only want to go if you go with me," Ella said. And then she raised her voice so her daddy wouldn't miss what she had to say. "You are going with me, Daddy. Aren't you?"

This chapter has been about teaching your daughter the importance of faith—of walking her through the steps to ensure that she knows God and has experienced the forgiveness and grace that has been offered through His Son, Jesus. But your daughter needs something from you. She needs the arms of her father securely wrapped around her as she pushes off into the unknown. You need to go too.

In his admonition specifically directed to fathers, the apostle Paul employs a word that is used in this particular tense only one time—this time—in the New Testament. It's the word *bring*, and it looks a lot like the picture we can see of Christopher, his arms wrapped tightly around his little girl, getting ready to embark on their dangerous journey. "Bring [your children] up with the discipline and instruction that comes from the Lord."[1]

This chapter will talk about faith. But this is not something you "send" your daughter to. It's not even good enough for you to "take" her. Instead, you wrap your arms around her and "bring" your girl to the Lord. Whatever this journey down the slide looks like for our daughters, you and I are right there too.

THE GUY OVER THERE WITH PINKEYE

Given a choice, I'd rather not attend "benefit" parties or donor banquets—and I don't mean that I don't enjoy getting together with friends for dinner. Bobbie and I love that. What I'm referring to are the ones where people invite you and your wife after they've "bought a table and would love for you to be our guests." Sometimes we're even assured that "it's not a fundraiser."

Run for your life. It's a trap.

Seriously, I do appreciate the work of so many worthy ministries, and I know that donor meals are their favorite strategy for telling their story and passing the hat. It's only that they're not my first choice for spending an evening out.

Then there are the neighborhood parties. When we transplanted from Tennessee to Florida in the year 2000, we found a home in a wonderful little community. By "little," I mean there are only 39 homes—just about what you might expect in Florida, except there are no shuffleboard courts. Very quickly after moving here, Bobbie and I made friends with the folks in the hood. All of them. I even joined the board of directors and, as of this writing, have been the neighborhood president for 12 of the past 14 years. Getting so involved in a neighborhood was a brand-new thing. Now, we have not only attended our neighborhood parties, but we've also hosted most of them.

In fact, if any of my former neighbors in Illinois or Texas or Tennessee are reading this, you cannot believe what you just read. Truthfully, I am very sorry that I didn't get involved before. My bad. Sure, we knew the families who were directly adjacent to our house, across the street, or—in the case of our last house in Nashville—around the cul-de-sac. They became close friends. But because I had chosen not to know anyone from farther away, neighborhood parties were basically a groaner. I went only because of a nagging sense of Christian obligation and because of Bobbie.

I am married to an outgoing person. Functions that feature lots of people, even strangers, energize her. On the other hand, I'm essentially a shy person. Even though I really do my best to be sincerely friendly, crowds drain my energy. Over the years, I've learned not to be shy in most situations. But given a choice, I'd rather spend the evening with Bobbie, our family, a few close friends, or just plain alone.

Back in the day, every conversation at those neighborhood parties where I knew no one had a similar ring to it. Question one: "Okay, so which house do you live in?" Answer: "The two-story at the end of Roantree Drive." Question two: "And what do you do?" Answer: The shortest description possible of what I did for a living.

After I had answered those questions as many times as I could possibly handle, I looked for my wife and begged her to come home with me or even to let me go home alone. Now that I think about it, the upside of a neighborhood party was that I actually could walk home.

Occasionally at one of those gatherings, someone would find out that I teach a Sunday school class. He'd ask which church we attend, and then he'd make a valiant attempt to identify with this "religious" person he had just encountered.

"You know, my second cousin married a guy whose next-door neighbor has a sister-in-law, and I think she's one of those." Then he'd add, "I've heard she's such a nice person." Yeah, but she probably kills chickens with her bare hands during full moons.

Once your poor neighbor had made this point of "religious" contact, he was off to get another drink and find someone normal. Someone who didn't have pinkeye.

Okay, what I've just told you is a slight exaggeration. But it's the way I used to feel about parties where I didn't know most of the guests. And, I'm afraid, it's the way lots of nonreligious people feel about bumping into Christians at parties.

I remember many years ago when Billy Graham was invited to make an appearance on *The Tonight Show*. He was always the first guest. Johnny Carson would be respectful and kind. Dr. Graham would also be respectful and kind. Then, as soon as the brief conversation was over, Johnny would say regretfully, "Unfortunately, Dr. Graham cannot be with us for the whole show." Then turning to his preacher guest, he'd extend his hand. "But it was *certainly* a pleasure having you with us tonight!"

Pleasant and sincere handshakes were exchanged, and Dr. Graham was gone. Then the real fun started.

THE ASTRO-BORING-DOME

In the late seventies, I took my family for a visit to the Astrodome in Houston. Opened in 1965, it was the first completely enclosed, domed stadium. Walking into a building that size was unbelievable—*indoor* baseball. No way. I remember gazing at the superstructure in absolute amazement. I also remember asking the guide if pop flies wouldn't just bounce off that ceiling.

She assured me they rarely get that high.

As part of the tour, she led our group into a small theater for a multimedia show. We were treated to a look at how the Astrodome was built—my favorite part—and how many different kinds of activities it could hold. We saw great action shots of rodeos, baseball games, tractor pulls (we were in Texas, remember), football games, and rock concerts.

The music behind these slides was exciting and loud. We got the idea that this building certainly did hold a lot of thrilling and fun events.

Then the music faded into what sounded like an old hymn, played by the lovely minister's wife with her hair pulled back in a bun, making music on a manual-pump organ in some clapboard country church. Over this nice, unobtrusive, and flat music, the announcer lowered his voice like a golf announcer at a funeral and told us that the Astrodome is so versatile that *it's even used for religious services.*

I remember feeling sick. *Why,* I thought, *isn't faith seen as just a normal part of life? Why do they have to drop the fun out of the music and portray Christians as uncolorful? Compared to the rest of life, basically boring?*

It's why neighbors often walked away after finding out that I went to church. But driving away from the Astrodome that day, Bobbie and I made a simple resolve: We will be happy about telling people that we are Christians. And we will demonstrate our faith with winsomeness and the enthusiasm it deserves. I will begin to show our daughters how to love our neighbors and do a better job of serving them. While they still had plenty of years left in our home, Missy and Julie began seeing us treat our love for God as part of our daily routine, not some clumsy diversion from real life.

So that's what we did. And by the time we had moved to Florida, we were full-on neighbor lovers. This has been a wonderful change, but I do wish I had done a better job of making our home an outpost for Christ when our girls were babies.

A Daughter Who Loves God

As when Ella asked her daddy to go down the scary slide with her, your task as a dad is to be an example of what it really looks like to love God and love others. To go first. Then you can bring her along. The primary job of a Christian dad is to build a little girl into a well-balanced woman who, like you, also loves God. And she arrives at this place when she fully understands how God feels about her.

Do You "Like" Me?

Forgive me for another quick visit to antiquity . . . my childhood. Until this point, I have not confessed to you that my wife, Bobbie, was not my first romantic love. It's true. Long before I ever knew she existed, I was thoroughly smitten by a woman. Her name was Cathy Roan, and we were both in the fourth grade.

As clearly as if I had done it last week, I remember gathering up my courage and writing Cathy a note. In it, I told her of my affection for her. (I don't think I actually used the word *love*.) And at the end of the note, I wrote a fill-in-the-blank question: "Do you like me? Please answer here." And then I made a short, straight line so she would know exactly where to write her answer.

I handed the note to Cathy the first thing in the morning after arriving at Whittier School. And for the remainder of the morning, I didn't hear a single thing Mrs. Sands said in class. My brain was on that little blank space at the end of my question.

Class was dismissed for the morning. I was getting my things ready to walk home for lunch. Cathy walked by my desk and handed me the note. I sat there at my desk until the room was completely empty and then slowly, deliberately, opened each fold. To my glorious delight, Cathy had written yes in that open space. In that moment, I was an Olympian who had just broken the world's record. I was a politician and my opponent had just conceded. I was in heaven.

Right now, more than 55 years after unfolding that note and read-ing Cathy's answer, I am vividly recalling that moment. Cathy Roan "liked" me.

Because of the untold and massive reach of social media, your daughter—and you—are putting notes in the hands of hundreds (thousands?) of people with a fill-in-the-blank space. We are wondering if all these people "like" us. Do they approve? Would they like us more if we acted a certain way? Or if we used a different language? Or if we "like" what they "like."

The most powerful, life-altering truth your daughter will ever encounter is this one. God "likes" her. Every morning when she opens her eyes, her first thought can be, *God has clicked the "like" button*. And she will have learned this from you because, even as a grown-up, you fully understand the power of this truth. God "likes" you.

So how do you get to the place where your daughter knows God and learns to "like" this One who "likes" her more than she could ever know?

Here are some ideas.

Bring her to church

The suggestions on the next few pages about the spiritual well-being of your daughter and her daddy are going to presume something. It's so basic that I'm tempted not to include it because I'm sure you already know about this one and I don't have any interest in insulting your intelligence. But just in case you need a bump, let me just go ahead and get it out of the way.

If you try to do this faith thing with your daughter without bringing her to church with you, you are making a terrible mistake. Said another way, please make churchgoing a non-negotiable with your daughter.[2]

In your Bible, two institutions are established and given special recognition. Way back in the book of Genesis, right after God creates a woman from the man's rib, He puts them together in a thing we now call marriage.

So the Lord God caused the man to fall into a deep sleep;
    and while he was sleeping, he took one of the man's ribs and
    then closed up the place with flesh. Then the Lord God made

a woman from the rib he had taken out of the man, and he brought her to the man.

The man said,

"This is now bone of my bones
and flesh of my flesh;
she shall be called 'woman,'
for she was taken out of man."
That is why a man leaves his father and mother and is united to
  his wife, and they become one flesh.[3]

Marriage—family—is the first celebrated institution.

The name of the second sacred institution comes from the lips of the Son of God. During one of their quiet getaways at a secluded place called Caesarea Philippi, Jesus talked to His closest friends about this special thing that happens every week in your neighborhood.

I will build *my church, and the gates of Hades will not
overcome it.*[4]

The day she was born, your daughter became a member of your family. As soon as possible, she needs to join another family—a "covenant family" . . . the church—and she'll be able to do this because you will bring her.[5]

Not long ago, my son-in-law Christopher asked me to help him build a small platform. He had recently suspended his career in the corporate world and joined our Julie in her candle business. The purpose of this little platform was to hold a "melter" that held a substantial quantity of liquid, hot soy wax for making candles.

The morning before Christopher and I were going to build the platform, we talked to the melter's manufacturer, an inventor named

Jason whom I've only met by phone. He was very helpful in telling us the required dimensions for the surface—four by five feet—and how high the platform needed to be from the ground—35 inches.

"How heavy is the melter when it's full?" I asked, preparing to take another run at a very important question. "How many pounds does the platform need to be able to hold?"

"One thousand pounds," Jason replied immediately.

"One thousand pounds?" I repeated, just in case I had misunderstood.

"Yes, one thousand pounds."

My brain came to a screeching halt. I was being asked to create something that, if it came crashing down with the tank of molten wax, could cause serious injuries to people I really loved—and make a horrendous mess.

After saying good-bye to Jason, I retrieved a sharp pencil from my drawer and took a yellow legal pad from the corner of my desk. My plan was to build this structure so it would be able to safely support a thousand pounds . . . plus a man—my granddaughters' daddy—standing on it next to the melter.

I'm no engineer, but I'm confident that the platform that Christopher and I built the next day could hold more than *two* thousand pounds. Maybe *three*. This was no time to take a chance.

Bringing your daughter to church is like building a platform for her life. On it will stand her network of friends who will influence her, her first exposure to grown-ups other than her parents, and spiritual instruction that will support what she has already learned from you.

If I had chosen to use two-by-fours instead of four-by-fours, would the wax melter platform have been strong enough? Maybe. But this was no time for taking a foolish risk. The platform needed to be stronger than it ever needed to be, so Christopher and I brought out the heavy stuff.

The spiritual platform your children stand on must meet the same, much-stronger-than-they-even-need-to-be standards. This is exactly why Bobbie and I brought our daughters to church. Combined with our promise to make our home a place of refuge and strength for her spiritual development, this platform gave us a chance to spend less time carping about the "dos and don'ts" of life—which we'll talk about in some detail in the next chapter—and more time enjoying our life together.

Thank God for her conception

In the first chapter, I talked about how surprised we were when we discovered that we—mostly Bobbie—were pregnant. Looking back on how I felt about receiving that news makes me smile now. But it was no laughing matter. I'm picturing a guy on the front row of a roller coaster as it descends that first slope. His eyes are wide open, his hair is blowing straight back, and his grip on the bar in front of him could not be released with a tire iron. You get the picture.

However, once I was able to catch my breath, Bobbie and I resolved that we were not only going to accept this news but celebrate it. In fact, we were going to thank God for this blessing.

Pregnancy is, for many people, something to be avoided. Billions of dollars are spent every year finding more and more reliable ways to keep from having children. But I believe that conception is something to be celebrated. Of all God's miracles, this one has been referred to for thousands of years as a specific sign of His *blessing*!

If you adopted your daughter, her conception is no less spectacular than if you and your wife had conceived her yourselves. In fact, in your case, God made *two* important choices: "To whom should I send this new life, and to whom should I give the privilege of her nurture and growth?" In either case—natural or adopted—congratulations on being chosen as this girl's general contractor!

King David wrote one of the most important descriptions of this miracle in Psalm 139. He used the metaphor of being "knit together" to illustrate the way God forms and blends the delicate fibers of a developing baby. It's an incredible thing.

Thank God for sending this girl your way. She's living at your house on purpose. Celebrate the miracle of conception.

Publicly promise to build your daughter

Some churches hold a special ceremony called a baby dedication. Some christen or baptize infants. But for our conversation here, it's essentially the same thing: As her dad, you are publicly acknowledging that this little girl is a gift—on loan—from God. And you promise to bring her up in the faith.

You must do this in front of lots of people you know—people who, hopefully, love you enough to remind you of this promise; friends who would, at some later time, dare to challenge your activity when it seems to be drifting from this pledge.

The Book of Order that guides our particular denomination puts it this way: "Believing parents are encouraged to present their children for the sacrament of baptism, which should not be unnecessarily delayed. Sacraments are holy signs and seals of the Covenant of Grace and in part confirm our position with and in Christ and demonstrate to the world the visible difference between it and those who belong to the Church."[6]

In fact, when a baby is brought before our congregation, the minister asks the members to signify that they promise to "assist the parents in the child's Christian nurture" by raising their right hand or saying aloud, "We will." It's an acknowledgment that building the child's faith will be a covenant family effort.

When you bring your little girl to the front of your church, promising to be an example of a godly man and asking your friends to be examples as well, you're putting the world on notice: I'm going to be a Christian father, I need some help from you, and I expect us to hold each other accountable on this one.

Present your daughter to God publicly.

Teach your daughter to pray

If conversation between you and your daughter (chapter 4) is critical to effectively building your relationship with each other, teaching your daughter to talk to God will be just as essential in building a meaningful relationship with Him.

Should you feel inadequate about exactly how to do this, there are many wonderful books that will be of help to you. But regardless of how you go about it, teach your daughter to pray. Show her how to do this out loud. Teach her by praying with and for her.[7]

Several years ago, our older daughter was teaching fifth grade at a Christian school in Charlotte. Classes would begin each day with a prayer time. Missy asked each student for requests, and then she would invite anyone to be a part of the prayer time—to pray out loud.

One morning, a boy began praying for his dog. He asked God to keep his dog, Rascal, from getting run over by cars on the busy street where he and his family lived. Then he asked the Lord to help Rascal get rid of his ringworm. This is only humorous, of course, if you're neither Rascal nor the ringworm.

What fun to hear that a child is so comfortable with God that he can bring his most important concerns boldly to God's attention.

Here are four guidelines to help you with teaching your girl to pray:

1. Begin with praise and thank-You's. When you pray with your daughter, help her to always begin by thanking God for His goodness. If she's young when you start this, you're going to hear God get thanked for a whole lot of interesting things: birds, iPads, flowers, Grandma, a new box of Honey Smacks cereal.[8] And that's okay. Let her roll. The older she gets, the more meaningful these "thank-You's" will become. You're helping her to see that everything she has—including life itself—is a precious gift from God's hand.

2. Follow with "Please forgive me's." You probably won't have too much difficulty with this, since most little girls have a great deal of sensitivity about their own shortcomings. But it's still important that you help her identify specific "forgive me's." "Forgive me for being selfish and not sharing my toys with Jennifer" when she's three will translate to seeking God's forgiveness when life gets a lot more complex and dangerous.

Warning: Teaching your daughter to confess her sins is not about beating her up with how awfully she has acted. Please hear me on this. This is simply a way for her to begin, at an early age, to notice those attitudes and actions in her life that are out of order and to understand her need for the cleansing forgiveness of a loving heavenly Father, experiencing the wonder of His grace.

And remember, she will be learning this from you. In other words, when you pray together she will hear you seeking God's forgiveness for your own thoughtless outbursts or ugly attitudes.

3. Offer requests. Like her list of "thank-You's," this might be a long one: "Bless Uncle Fred and Aunt Blanche, bless my dolls and teddy bears, bless my mommy and my daddy [Amen], bless my older sister in school, help Stephanie to get over the flu, help Daddy to let me have pierced ears and a cell phone, please give us a sunny day tomorrow for the picnic . . ." Again, it's okay. Let this roll. Your daughter is learning that God is a God of blessing—of good and perfect gifts.

4. End with "Thank You." And finally, it's a good idea to help her close the prayer with one more statement of "Thank You."

There you have it. Don't be embarrassed to actually *teach* this. If it means having her repeat phrases after you, that's okay. By listening to you pray, in no time she'll get the hang of it.

You've taught your daughter the importance of talking to God, and you've given her an example of what it sounds like. This is very good.

Hint: If you're looking for times to pray, there are two "for sures." One is at mealtimes. You may be thanking God only for the food and not going down a list of requests, but make this a habit. Three times a day, you're reminding your daughter of God's tangible goodness and blessing. The second "for sure" is bedtime. This will be the best place for you to take a little more time and walk through the four guidelines we just discussed.

Teach your daughter to pray.

Teach your daughter to sing

When it comes to teaching your child to sing, there are places you can go for help. If you "google" Christian songs for kids, you'll find plenty. Many of the "new songs" your daughter learns at church are terrific. Bobbie and I are partial to the old hymns, which is why, in 2003, she and her friend Joni Eareckson Tada created the book and CD called *Hymns for a Kid's Heart.* This was so well received that Bobbie and Joni did three more volumes over the next few years.

Two or three times through these songs, and your daughter will have them memorized. You'll hear her singing them to herself. As the words sink into her heart, they will be like reinforcing steel in the concrete of her character.

In addition to the songs she hears, you can also teach her little songs on your own. You can do this. Of course, there are the old stand-bys "Jesus Loves Me" and "Jesus Loves the Little Children."

There are also simple songs like "God Is So Good":

God is so good, God is so good, God is so good, He's so good to me.

Then there are verses you can add:

He gave us Grandma,
He gave us Grandma,

He gave us Grandma.
He's so good to me.

The possibilities are endless:

He gave us _____*(insert your daughter's name) . . .*
He gave us Mommy . . .
He gave us Daddy (my personal favorite) . . .

You might want to have your daughter learn some of the great old hymns of the church too. "Holy, Holy, Holy," "How Firm a Foundation," and "A Mighty Fortress Is Our God," for example, are filled with incredible truths.[9]

Music is going to be an important part of your daughter's life. It's the language of her generation, symbolizing the thinking of a culture. When she's old enough to navigate an iPod or tablet—probably while she's still in diapers—you're going to be concerned about her tastes in that musical "language." This is an almost universal situation. Dads are a little—or a lot—worried about their daughters' selection of music. So when your daughter is young, give her some of the really good stuff. It will help her as she makes musical judgments later.

Teach your daughter to sing.

Teach your daughter to give and serve

Spiritually speaking, there may not be a more important habit for your daughter to acquire than giving her money to the church and serving in ways that involve her. Again, this is something she's going to need to learn from you, so here are two ideas.

First, let your daughter see you put something in the offering plate every time it passes. Give her something to put into the offering when she's small. When she begins to earn her own money, be matter-of-fact about it, but remind her to give. There are many wonderful causes, such as caring for the poor around the world or inner-city ministries, that your daughter could give to, even if it's just a few pennies a week.

The Bible doesn't say there's anything wrong with money. What it clearly says is that it is foolish to *love* money. In fact, it warns that if we start loving our money, evil will have a superb chance to take root. (See 1 Timothy 6:10.) Showing your daughter how to give generously will demonstrate that you know how to hold your money with an open hand and refuse to fall in love with it.

Second, when your schedule allows, sign up yourself and your daughter when your church has special workdays or sends people on mission trips. In 1997, I took our daughter Julie to Central America. Just the two of us for a week in Guatemala. This was a very good idea. We visited families who lived in little dirt-floor huts. We sang to children whose only wardrobe was what they were wearing, and yet they were kids who found a great sense of joy in their hearts because they loved Jesus. We thought we were going to bless and encourage them. They blessed and encouraged us.

Teach your daughter to give and serve.

Buy her a Bible of her own

Many churches give children a Bible when they enter the third grade. There are often ceremonies in "big church" where the kids come forward to receive their Bibles. In most cases, these are grown-up Bibles, with page after page of difficult-to-read, tiny black words on white paper.

If that is literally her first Bible, you've missed a fantastic opportunity.

Although it may be only a symbol before she's old enough to read, having a Bible of her own will help her understand that, at any age, this faith can actually be hers. Again, a quick visit to a Christian bookstore or bookselling website (like ChristianBook.com) will help you find just the right Bible for her.

Give your daughter the pride of having her own Bible. And have her name imprinted on the outside if you can. It's *hers*. And when you read to your daughter, read out of *her* Bible. Let her understand that the Book she's carrying around is filled with wonderful truth—truth that can be her very own.

Teach your daughter Bible verses

I've waited until now to tell you about my mother. She went to heaven in 2010, but she was an angel long before she was transported.

One week during the summer of 1976, Bobbie and I asked my parents if they would take care of Julie while we vacationed in Missouri with friends. They said they'd be glad to.

We returned to my parents' house late on a Saturday afternoon, and after all the we-missed-you's and thanks-for-taking-care-of-Julie's were finished, my mother said, "Robert and Bobbie, Julie has something for you." I was expecting a watercolor or a raft made out of wooden Popsicle sticks. Wrong on both counts.

With a huge smile on her face, Julie turned toward us and began to recite:

A—"All we like sheep have gone astray."

B—"Be ye kind one to another."

C—"Children obey your parents, for this is the right thing to do."

D—"Don't fret or worry, it only leads to harm."

E—"Every good and perfect gift is from above . . ."[10]

Standing there in front of us, Julie recited 26 Bible verses, each beginning with a letter of the alphabet, all the way from "All we like sheep" to "Zacchaeus, you come down." We were stunned. We were also deeply grateful that my mother had planted those verses in our daughter's heart. Three months later, Julie turned two!

As we drove back to our house, Bobbie and I decided to keep it up. So we—Bobbie, mostly—helped the girls memorize lots and lots of Bible verses. In fact, she got so serious about it that she made a rule: No Bible, no breakfast.

Please believe me, this was all in fun. There were no morning furrowed brows or angry directives on this—"You memorize Ecclesiastes or you starve." We made a game of it—like checkers or slapjack.

I suppose we'll never know how important those verses have been in our girls' lives, but I do know King David promised that hiding God's Word in our hearts helps us defend against sin (see Psalm 119:11). That's a good reason all by itself, don't you think?

Pour the Scriptures into your daughter's heart.

Talk about God

On those never-go-on-errands-alone weekend trips to the Home Depot or Lowe's, when you're talking and patting your daughter's knee, include God. For example, as you're driving along and you see a pretty tree, say, "Oh, honey, look at the beautiful tree. Isn't God wonderful to have created something like that for us to enjoy?"

She'll say, "Yes, Daddy." And that'll be all.

Do not add anything to it. Please don't say, "You know, it's like Reverend Smith said on Sunday morning—at the eight-thirty worship service and again at eleven o'clock . . ."

> *Talk about God with your daughter as though knowing Him is a simple fact, not something strange or puzzling.*

That's not normal.

Just say something about God and then follow it with something ordinary like "Why don't you go ahead and tie your shoe so you don't trip over the laces when we get to the store?" Talk about God with your daughter as though knowing Him is a simple fact, not something strange or puzzling.

Give your daughter an extended Christian family

If your girl is young, begin praying that God will send her other Christian adults who will love her for free. These are people who love God, like you, but they're not teachers ("Did you finish your homework?"), coaches ("Take another lap"), extended family ("When your dad was little, he used to . . ."), or surrogate parents ("Clean your room").

These "free" adults will do almost as much to shape your daughter's life and thinking as you. There are lots of good places to find folks like this, but your church is the best. You can also locate these adults in Youth for Christ, Young Life, Fellowship of Christian Athletes, and many wonderful Christian summer camping programs. If you're really lucky, you'll find a Christian adult friend for your daughter right in your own neighborhood.

What you pray for is that these people will occasionally say to your daughter, "You know, your dad is right." That can be a powerful thing.

When we lived in Texas, Bobbie met Charlotte Mitchell at a Bible study. Although they didn't know each other well, Bobbie called Charlotte and asked if she and her husband would be able to take care of four-year-old Julie while we were out of town for a weeklong trade show. Charlotte agreed.

As it turned out, Charlotte and David Mitchell were gifts to us. The Christian attitudes and values they underscored in Julie's heart were priceless. Even today, more than 30 years later, the memory of her week with the Mitchells fills Julie with a reminder of what God can do in other families.

Give your daughter a Christian family beyond your own. You won't be sorry.

Give your daughter an opportunity to teach

If you visit a church nursery or preschool Sunday school class, you'll notice something. In addition to the regular adult teachers, there are also helpers. More often than not, these folks are charged with duties like picking up toys or taking the little ones to the potty.

Encourage your daughter, as soon as she's old enough, to volunteer for that kind of duty. As she works with the younger children, she'll find herself on the receiving end of honest inquiries about life. And relationships. And God. As your daughter works through answers for those inquisitive little minds, she'll be sealing her own ideas and thinking about such things.

Being a "teacher" will also give her good questions to bring to you about the unique claims of Jesus. Because our world is "getting smaller," it won't be long until your daughter is exposed to people of other faiths and worldviews. As soon as she stumps you with a tough question (you won't have to wait long for this), you can search for an answer together. Biblical faith is defensible, and with a plentiful supply of love and grace, questions can be answered.

Give your girl an opportunity to learn by teaching.

Bless your daughter

Depending on your spiritual training and background, this one may take some getting used to, but please hear me out. The Old Testament is filled with stories about fathers giving a blessing to their children. In fact, one of the best-selling Christian books in the 1980s was *The Blessing*, written by Dr. Gary Smalley and Dr. John Trent. In a nutshell, the concept is that parents have a responsibility to provide verbal blessings to their children.

Centuries ago, people would not have had to be reminded of this concept. It was a common thing. In fact, people spoke blessings to each other when they met on the sidewalk. "Peace to you" was a lot more common than "Hey, what's up?"

Giving and receiving blessings is just a good idea.

I have no idea how this got started in our family, but for many years, after we say good-bye to our daughters, we've added, "The Lord be with you." They return the statement with "The Lord be with you, too."

In a moment of verbal interchange, we've given each other a blessing. It's a comforting and inspiring way to say good-bye.

Verbally bless your daughter.

Give your daughter an awe for God

Think about this: When you and your daughter are talking to or about God, you are literally referring to the eternal Creator of the universe . . . the One who spoke everything into existence.[11] This Person is not only more important than other people, such as your favorite actor or professional athlete, but after He ordered the cosmos to exist, He *made* people, first using dust as His raw material.

Remind your daughter of God's majesty by an occasional mention of His creative genius. A colony of ants crossing the sidewalk in single file, or the inner beauty of a single flower—God did this.

Bobbie and I have close friends who were hiking in Colorado a few years ago. They came upon an old, abandoned mining town. In their exploration, they came across a rusted-out piece of excavating equipment. Looking closely, they found a small plaque that identified the manufacturer: the Frick Company, Waynesboro, Pennsylvania. They took a cell phone picture of this and sent it to me. In the forties, while he pastored a little church in this same town, my dad worked at the Frick Company. The photo on my phone sent chills down my arms. These friends had found something in the underbrush, 2,000 miles from where it had been built. The machine was forged in steel, and its creator was emblazoned on it.

An awe for God includes the goose bumps that come when you and your daughter realize that creation is exactly that—something created. Billions of stars and the veins on a fly's wing. A soaring bird on a windy day and the face of a puppy. These things will remind both of you that God is truly—and here's an overused word that fits perfectly this time—awesome.

Let her know that when you pray, sometimes you kneel down because you're so honored to be in the presence of an awesome God. Even though you are a daddy and your daughter is under your authority, it's good for her to know that you also have an Authority. You would never dare to live without worshiping a loving God to whom you answer.

Every once in a while let her join you on your knees. Begin your prayer by thanking God for His wonder. His creation. Tell Him, out loud, that you are amazed at who He is. Your daughter will get the picture.

Day after day, I do my best to speak to God, the God who created the heavens and the earth. It's part of my routine. As they were growing up, I helped my daughters speak to Him. It's an overwhelming thing—being in the presence of this kind of power and perfection and greatness.

The most important thing we can do to help develop a daughter's personal faith is to give her a glimpse of what it is to actually *be* in God's presence. Once that's firmly planted in her heart, many other troublesome issues will take care of themselves—including her conduct, which we'll talk about in the next chapter.

Give your daughter an awe for God.

BUILDING A HOUSE FOR GOD

In October 1982, on an unusually balmy evening, Bobbie and I were on our way to a weekly Bible study with a few other couples from our church. As we got closer to our friends' house, we noticed a yellow glow in the sky not too far from where we were. Hopelessly curious person that I am, I took a little detour.

Over the years, I had seen buildings on fire. Mostly I had seen smoke coming from upstairs windows, with a few flames here and there. But this night, I saw a house on *fire.* The flames were shooting 50 feet into the air. The crackling and popping sounded like something from camp, only on a much grander scale. Sparks completely filled the night sky.

Standing on the curb across from the inferno and feeling the radiated heat from the conflagration, I remember thinking, *Whoever lives in this house won't sleep tonight. How could they? In a few minutes, their beloved home will be completely gone.*

Regardless of who built your house, it has something in common with mine. They've been built, for the most part, with flammable materials. The careless use of matches or a gas stove that blows up will turn our homes into towering mountains of flame.

In the Psalms, King David made an important observation about your family's "contractor": "Unless the LORD builds the house, the builders labor in vain" (127:1).

Building your daughter—and your home—with a solid faith is about using materials that are completely "fire-retardant." The eternal values that come with directing your daughter toward a God who loves her will help you build a home that lasts.

Builder's Checklist

1. *Make your faith "normal."* One of the most important things you can do is to make your faith a part of your daily routine.
2. *Teach your daughter to pray.* Go ahead and teach her, just as you taught her to tie her shoes. A prayer should include:
   a. Praise and "thank-You's"
   b. "Please forgive me's"
   c. Requests
   d. One last "Thank You"
3. *Review the ways to build godly character in your daughter:*
   - Bring her to church.
   - Thank God for the miracle of your daughter's conception and birth.
   - Publicly promise to build and nurture her.
   - Teach your daughter to pray.
   - Teach your daughter to sing.
   - Teach your daughter to give and serve.
   - Buy her a Bible of her own.
   - Teach your daughter Bible verses.

- Talk about God.
- Give your daughter an extended Christian family.
- Give your daughter an opportunity to teach.
- Bless your daughter.
- Give her an awe for God.

4. *Let her teach you.* Helping to build a solid faith in your daughter will have a profound influence on your own faith. Among other effects, as she gets older, you'll discover why Jesus commended the little children for the depth of their faith, because she'll teach you!

CONDUCT

You Be the Judge

> *When you go out into the world, watch out*
> *for traffic, hold hands, and stick together.*
> —ROBERT FULGHUM

Let's say that you call me tomorrow morning to tell me you're going to be in my town next weekend. You ask if I might be free on Saturday afternoon to go for a drive, taking you on a little tour of Orange County, Florida. There are lots of things to see here.[1] I say it would be fine for you to come by. We set a time, I give you directions to my house, we say good-bye, and we hang up.

The following Saturday, at the appointed time, you pull into my driveway, and since you're not still in high school, you actually get out of your car and meet me at the front door. We exchange greetings, I grab a light jacket, and we walk back down the sidewalk toward your car.

When we get to your car, I mention that I'd prefer riding in the backseat. Thinking it's a strange suggestion, you try to talk me out of it. But since this is my story and I'm making the rules, I prevail.

As we back out of the driveway, you feel silly—like a cab driver in your own car. You've never gone out with a friend who was sitting in the backseat. *This really feels weird*, you think.

Leaving my neighborhood, I ask if you've ever driven around my town before. You say you haven't. I tell you I'll be happy to show you around. *But why is he sitting in the backseat?* you continue to wonder. You take a deep breath and do your best to get this unusual setup out of your mind.

When we come to the first stop sign, you pause. "Which way should I turn?" you ask.

"Oh, you just go ahead," I reply.

"But I don't know where I'm going," you counter.

"That's okay," I say. "I'll let you know."

You take a moment, look left and right, and then turn left. I don't say anything.

In a mile or so, we come to a traffic light. It's red. While we're sitting there, waiting for the green, you ask, "Which way now?"

"You go ahead," I say. "I'll let you know."

The light turns green. Again you look left and right. Since most of the cars you're following turn left, you turn left too. *Left worked last time*, you reason, *so maybe it'll work again.*

But the moment the car clears the intersection after your left turn, I lean forward and slap the right side of your face with my open hand. Hard. The impact of the blow sends your sunglasses flying.

You're so shocked that it takes a minute for you to say anything. But you slow down, gather your composure—and your sunglasses—and glance over your shoulder. "What was that!" you exclaim.

"Wrong turn," I shoot back.

More than a little bewildered, you look for an opportunity to make a safe U-turn and head down the road in the correct direction.

For the next several hours, we tour my county. I never tell you where we're going or which way to turn at intersections. I only let you know, with my open hand, if you've made the wrong choice.

After a few hours, you have resolved that (a) this is the last time you're ever taking me on a drive, and (b) I'm a complete and worthless jerk. Good thinking on both accounts.

WELCOME TO THE WORLD OF BEING A KID

Admittedly, the scenario I've just walked you through is ridiculous. Who would ever do such a thoughtless and contemptuous thing?

How could I have expected you to do any better unless I had told you, in advance, where we were going and the best way to get there?

You're way ahead of me, aren't you? What I'm describing is the way many children feel as they grow up with parents who seem to know where their kids are supposed to go, but the only real directions they give are those painful physical or verbal "slaps" when the children make wrong choices. And although you and I would never be as brutal and unfair as I was in our story, I assure you that what I've described is not an uncommon way to explain what it sometimes *feels* like to be a kid.

Maybe you've seen the game Whac-A-Mole. It's another way to look at what your girl may be feeling when it comes to how she's supposed to act at your house. What you expect her to do. And what you expect her not to do. She's the mole and you're the whacker.[2]

THE ORDER IS INTENTIONAL

This chapter is about conduct—how your girl should act in certain situations. It's the seventh "thing you need to know to build a complete daughter," and it's purposely at the end of these seven chapters.

Even if we've got a high-spirited, strong-willed girl, setting rules for conduct should be our last concern.

Why? Because when we have problems to be solved, you and I want answers. And we want them right away. We buy books because we want answers. Right? *Hey, I paid good money for this book. Don't waste my time with philosophical drivel—just tell me what to do and what not to do.*

But even if we've got a high-spirited, strong-willed girl, setting rules for conduct should be our *last* concern. If we try to make it first on our list, we'll spend most of our time "slapping" from the backseat. Whacking the mole.

Let's review the last six chapters, but this time let's focus on how they relate, ultimately, to conduct.

1. Protection. Your role as the guiding and protecting "point person" in your girl's life is a given. You can't delegate it to anyone else. Even though this parenting thing is a partnership with your wife, your job as the protecting dad is irreplaceable. Early on, you discover that your daughter is susceptible to all sorts of dangers. Some are physical. Many are electronic. You must know when to parent and when to "de-parent"—when to step in to protect and when to let your daughter learn a lesson. Without an understanding of your role in protecting, you may not have understood why you must be the one to administer the guidelines of conduct.

2. Conversation. In every situation you encounter with your daughter, your ability to openly talk about it will be the greatest guiding "device" you could employ. Good conversation releases the internal, secret pressure that builds toward foolish or dangerous conduct. And don't forget: That good conversation is not possible if either of you has an electronic device in your hands. When you talk, if your daughter feels free to talk to you about what's really going on in her life, she'll hit the pause button on that thing in her hand—whatever it is—and engage with you.

3. Affection. Your girl must feel the enveloping security of your physical and emotional "arms." She must know your tender touch and your affirming words. And these must come from you at times when there's no direct connection between her conduct and your loving support. You are affirming her *person*, not her *performance*.

4. Discipline. Yes, this is about conduct. But it's about your conduct—personal discipline—in stark contrast to, or in support of, your attempts to be the disciplinarian. It's about toughness, consistency, and fairness. It's about your willingness to be "the bad guy" in order to build the gyroscope of discipline inside your daughter.

5. *Laughter.* More than anything else, fun-loving laughter helps you be real. It's the cornerstone in the developing friendship between you and your daughter. Laughter gives you something to look forward to—it's a holiday you and your girl take from the serious rigors of making rules and setting guidelines. Laughter gives balance to a tough-to-face world.

6. *Faith.* Your job is to usher your girl into the presence of an awesome God, helping her understand that the more she knows about Him—His justice and grace—the less emphasis there will need to be on conduct. And you are teaching her how to listen carefully to God's voice as He speaks to her. Like a relay runner, slowly but surely, you pass the spiritual baton from your hand to hers. Her life, from the time she's born until that trip down the aisle toward her groom or when she launches out on her own, is essentially the "exchange zone." Success in the dimension of faith is when your daughter is running, baton in hand, without you. The best for your daughter is not growing up to be what you want her to be. The best for her is growing up to be what God wants her to be.

BEGIN WITH THE END IN MIND

In the first chapter, you read about Cousin Larry's Construction Company and the artist's rendering of a finished building project. That illustrated the importance of always focusing on the finished product rather than the often-frustrating details of the day to day.

Talking about conduct is almost always unpleasant, even dangerous. Without any context, it can sound as if you're placing conditions on your love: "I will love you more when your conduct is acceptable."

However, as you build your daughter, your challenge is the same one that Cousin Larry's Construction Company faced: focusing not on the process (conduct) but on the payoff (completeness). Begin with the end in mind.

Speak to the goal you're attempting to reach

In chapter 5, I warned against complimenting other girls in areas where your daughter could never measure up—for example, in physical attributes like hair color and body shape. But the same principle can be applied from a positive point of view.

Compliment others in areas where you *want* your daughter to excel—in places where she *can* achieve. For example, instead of talking about another girl's hair color or stature, say to that child, "I noticed how polite you were when you spoke to your mother. That is so good." Say this in your daughter's presence.

Your goal is to build a respectful and well-mannered daughter, and that's something she knows she can achieve. So you give her a glimpse of your priorities through your observation of another child.

Warning: After complimenting another child, don't turn to your girl and say anything about *her* conduct. Do *not* compare her manners to those of the girl you've just spoken about. If her conduct doesn't measure up at the moment, she'll get the message. No further analysis will be necessary from you.

Or you can look for opportunities to catch your daughter doing something right: "Thank you for helping Mrs. Jamison with baby Mary. She told me how much she appreciates your kindness."

You are painting a picture of what you have in mind for your own daughter, and you're "hanging" that picture in a place where she can see it. You're putting a high value on achievable goals, but you're letting her draw that conclusion herself.

This is a powerful thing.

Focus on negative consequences and positive rewards

You have four useful allies in illustrating the inescapable truths of cause and effect: your own experience, the experiences of your friends and acquaintances, the daily news, and rewards.

Regarding your own experiences, there's no need to go into the sordid details. But you can usually talk openly about the unhappy *result* of past foolishness.

And again, there's no need to finish the story with, "So see, honey, this is what will happen if you do such and such." Don't insult her by stating an obvious conclusion. Let her draw her own. It will make a much stronger impact on her if she has to think about it herself.

The experiences of your friends and acquaintances also provide a helpful backdrop for your reasons for good conduct.

Then, let your daughter see (some of) the daily news. Because news organizations are most interested in building their audience, they often put the most shocking or tragic stories at the front of their news shows or web posts. The message to your daughter will be clear: Activity always has results. Foolish conduct creates unhappiness and chaos. To avoid such consequences, avoid such conduct.

Your other ally is rewards. When your daughter is small, you'll be amazed at what she'll do for a page of stickers or a trip to her favorite frozen-yogurt place. If her conduct warrants such a reward, she'll get it. If it doesn't, she won't.

Warning: Be certain that the rules are clear. "If you do thus and so, you'll get thus and so." Make the completion of the task and the achievement of the reward objective and completely up to her. When she's young, you may even want to post a list of her desired activities and potential rewards on the refrigerator. Also, be absolutely certain you have your wife's support on this, as well as on any other issues related to conduct. Don't present the plan to your daughter until there's unanimity among "the judges."

Help your daughter search for her own gifts

When I was growing up, the areas where a girl could excel were limited—primarily music and academics. So the valedictorians and soloists at the commencement ceremony were usually girls. Happily, we now live in a culture where the possibilities for your daughter's personal achievement are almost inexhaustible.

Your job is to help her find that special area where she can be a winner.

King Solomon said it this way, "Train up a child in the way he [or she] should go . . ." (Proverbs 22:6, NASB). In other words, your job is to mentor, or coach, your daughter according to her own particular bent, or skill set. The personal satisfaction of achievement, coupled with the accolades of her friends, will do more to shape her conduct than any list you could ever create, even if your list were the best ever conceived.

To do this, you'll need to expose your girl to many different options when she's young: music, dance, sports, art, collectibles, drama, and so on. You'll discover that what you loved or achieved as a youngster may not interest her at all. Do your best to affirm every possibility—unless, of course, she develops an interest in building explosives in your garage.

Once she lands on her own specialty, she'll blossom.

TECHNOLOGY

I wrote the original edition of this book in 1996. Back then I could not have even comprehended what was about to happen with high-speed Internet, smartphones, and tablets. Technology is screaming past us at speeds you and I cannot imagine. In fact, the publisher had better hurry and get this book to press, or what I just said about smartphones and tablets will be obsolete!

I'm smiling at the thought of how this public service announcement would have sounded in the mid-nineties: "Don't text and drive."

I'm imagining that I would have wondered why I shouldn't take one of my college textbooks in the car with me and why I would have been tempted to read it while I was driving. Hardly.

The world has changed, and all these new devices and gadgets are wonderful. But a chapter on conduct cannot overlook the need for a dad like you to deal with the impact of technology on your daughter.

Of all the joys of advanced technology, I guess my favorite is the global positioning system (GPS). You probably already know this, but GPS was originally developed by the military. Then in the 1980s it was made available for ordinary folks. It's amazing.

I used to be a map guy. From the time I was a young boy, I was fascinated with following our family car trips on a big map that we'd unfold in the car. I can remember tracing the road we were on with my finger. Because the whole map was in front of me, I had a larger sense of where we were. When I became a driver, I still loved maps. Our glove compartment was full of them. I was fascinated with geography.

In addition to the satisfaction of seeing where we were in the context of the whole state, I enjoyed having maps that kept me from getting lost. If there's a sensation I despise, it's the one that starts with a grinding feeling in my stomach. The one that whispers, *Hey man, you have no idea where you are. You're as lost as last year's Easter egg. What are you going to do now?*

I hate that feeling. It's one that I wanted to prevent at all cost. So I used road maps to help me know exactly where I was and where I was going.

Now, thanks to my smartphone and the system in my car that I sometimes use as a backup, I have the assurance that I will never get lost again. The desperate need to do whatever I can to keep from getting off track is no longer there. Technology has given me a sense of security about where I am. But this is a false sense of security. Truth be known, GPS has ruined my sense of direction. Okay, so I can get from point A to point B safely. But so what. Ask me if I'm northwest or southeast of the city, right side up or upside down, and I will confess that I have no idea. Back in the day, I used to know. But now I don't know. I have traded in my understanding of where I am on a map of the whole state for a little lighted screen and a voice that tells me to make the next turn in 500 feet. The powerful motivation that I used to feel in order to avoid getting lost is no longer the prevailing fear.

Because your daughter can look at that thing in the palm of her hand and find an answer to any imaginable question, or communicate in a split second with anyone on the planet, she thinks she understands how the world works. She doesn't.

Technology has given your daughter a false sense of security. Just because she can tell you in a moment if it's going to rain in Hong Kong tomorrow or who signed the Declaration of Independence or who starred in *Gone with the Wind*, she thinks that she's intelligent and wise. She can access amazing information almost immediately—and probably faster than you can (those buttons on the phone were not made for fingers the size of yours and mine)—so she has the capacity of believing a horrible lie: "I'm smarter than my dad, so I don't need to listen to him. He's old and slow and stupid, and I have this little gadget that helps me outrun him whenever I want."

Your daughter may know how to get from point A to point B, but she still doesn't know where she is or where she's going. Smartphone or not, she needs you to help her with these things.

Of course, there are many dangers to technology. There are scam artists who can steal your passwords, peers who engage in cyber-bullying, and predators who can follow your daughter. All of these are real concerns to guard against. But I suspect that the greatest peril of technology is the whisper in your little girl's ear that she doesn't really need her dad.

The best part of technology is how helpful it is, used properly. But used improperly, she can play games on her device that steal precious minutes—hours—from you. Our daughter Julie regularly admonishes her daughters that their smartphones are a tool, not a toy.

And Missy encourages her children to put down their devices and "be fully present."

Both of these encouragements are very wise.

Okay, Okay, But What About "the List" of Dos and Don'ts?

Being a great daddy is a lot like being a successful manager in business. Your relationship with your subordinates is sound. There's trust and mutual support. They know exactly what they're supposed to do. Finally, you're close enough to the work to see—I didn't say "meddle in"—how well they're doing day to day, just in case there's a need for some midcourse correction.

In reading through the following list of dos and don'ts, remember the wisdom of one of my favorite motivational speakers, the late Zig Ziglar: To be an effective parent, you must let your children know what you *expect* from them, and then you must be close enough to the action to be able to regularly *inspect* their work. Your success will depend on your ability to communicate clearly what you want them to do and your diligence in making sure your daughter is completing her task.

Now, because every dad needs some help with specific situations, here are a few suggestions. Those that I believe may be "hills worth dying on" are marked with an asterisk (*).

Chores*

We know two things for sure about Cousin Larry's Construction Company. First, his workers knew their assignments. Whatever their particular trade—carpenter, electrician, plumber—they showed up with the right tools. But second, they did not do their thing by themselves. Their task, whatever its nature, was accomplished alongside other workers.

To give your daughter chores—family-helping assignments—is to give her a gift. (It's not necessary to refer to chores as gifts you are giving her. When she's married and has children of her own, she'll completely get this part.) You are teaching your daughter how to work and the joys of doing her assignments well.

In this scenario, another member of her work crew may be a sibling. But, for sure, one of her work colleagues is her dad. You.

When you were a kid, you may have never seen your dad do any household tasks. Some back then called it "woman's work." This expression is as old school and obsolete as "eight-track tape" and "buggy whip."

Yes, your daughter needs to have her own chores to do, but there also needs to be a sense that she's not doing all her assignments by herself. Our son-in-law, who spent some time playing professional soccer and whose last name is Tassy, calls doing chores together "Team Tassy." And even though it really *is* work—vacuuming the house, folding clothes, doing the dinner dishes—Christopher does his best to come alongside and help the helper. He often turns on some music and tries to make the work fun.

Successful and happy families are a lot of work. Giving your daughter her own assignments—chores—is giving her the joy and privilege of being on a winning team.

Disobedience*

Depending on your daughter's nature, her "ability" to disobey may come at an early age. You'll know she understands obedience—and disobedience—when you've asked her to do or not do something and she hesitates and then does the opposite of what you asked.

Before she could walk, our baby Missy was crawling across the living-room floor toward the fireplace. I said, "No, Missy." She stopped and turned toward me as if to say, *Are you talking to me? No, you must be referring to some other crawling child about to do something dangerous.* Then she continued to crawl toward the fire.

I quickly ran to her, picked her up, sat her on my lap, got her attention, and took an extended sequence of light swats at her diapered, well-protected bottom. She immediately cried, knowing I was displeased with what she had done. At that very early age, my daughter understood that disobedience is unacceptable. No discussion necessary.

In chapter 6, I talked about "the first time." Obeying is what the first time is about. Please don't wait on this one. Make it swift and sure every time. It won't be long before you will rarely have to punish for disobedience. The message will have been transmitted and received loud and clear: Don't disobey.

Long after our daughters were grown and gone, I was sitting in a doctor's waiting (and waiting and waiting) room, wondering if perhaps his assistant had meant 2:30 *tomorrow* afternoon.

While I waited, I people-watched. There were folks with bandages on their arms or faces, people with colds sniffling away, and a few who didn't look sick at all. I made up possible reasons for why they were there. Right next to me was a little girl, probably two years old. Her daddy was on the other side of her, apparently having drawn the short straw on taking his daughter to the doctor.

To say this girl was fidgety would be an understatement. She never stopped moving. She'd sit on the seat, move to the arm of the chair on my side, and then switch to the arm on her daddy's side. Then she'd get down off the chair and crawl under it, looking for something, anything, to do.

After every one of her movements, this curly-headed perpetual-motion machine would hear her father say, "No, Ashley." She'd move; he'd say no. She would stop for one second, move again, and he'd say no again.

Was this disobedience? Technically, yes. Was it punishable? If you're talking about punishing the little girl, absolutely not. Why? Because she was literally incapable of doing *nothing*. So, instead of her dad droning on "No, no, no," he should have said, "Here, Ashley, let's play a game."

One of our favorites at such moments was "B. B. Bumblebee, I see something you don't see." With no props, we could keep a two-year-old busy for . . . well . . . several minutes! You go first and say, "B. B. Bumblebee, I see something you don't see, and it is . . . red." Then you give your daughter a chance to look around the room and guess what red thing you might be looking at. When she gets it right, it's her turn.

Crying

There are two kinds of crying when your daughter is still very young. One means "I am legitimately hungry, wet, or injured." That kind of crying is understandable and, of course, acceptable. Do whatever is necessary to remove the problem: Feed her, change her, or soothe her injury.

Then there's the other kind of crying that means "I'm ticked off, I'm not getting my way, and this is how I'm going to get a little attention around here." We ignored this kind of crying until it went away, or we punished if it didn't. That, in turn, created a reason to cry—spanking—so then it could be soothed.

As your daughter grows, keep the rules about crying the same: Crying is permissible—actually, welcomed—for legitimate reasons like hurt feelings, physical injury, sorrow. But crying should not be an acceptable method of gaining leverage to get her way or send a message to her parents.

In most states, it's illegal to flash your car's headlights for any reason other than to signal some kind of legitimate distress. I had a friend in high school who once saw a speed trap—a motorcycle cop with what looked like a hair dryer aimed at oncoming traffic. It was not a hair dryer.

My friend decided to alert drivers on the other side of the road that they were being watched. Unfortunately for him, there was a speed trap on his own side of the highway in another mile or so, and when the policeman saw him flashing his lights, he pulled him over.

"Who do you think you are, Paul Revere?" was all the highway patrolman said to my friend. Then he gave him a stiff ticket.

Crying, like flashing headlights, should only be for signaling distress. Don't let it be used any other way.

Whining

Assuming there are no medical reasons to cause whining and pouting, they're usually a result of simple boredom. They often follow mindlessly staring at the television or computer screens for hours on end.

When your daughter comes to you, talking with that annoying, high-pitched whine, tell her first that, as my wife used to say, "I can't understand what you're saying when you talk like that. Talk to me in a big-girl voice."

Then, two actions usually bring about a solution: (1) Turn off the electronic thing, and (2) help her find something to do. Get creative. Have her help you in the garden. If you're a cook, have her help you in the kitchen. Take her to the store with you. Help her start a leaf collection. Buy some watercolors and paintbrushes.

Get her good books to read and curl up together.

Once you've done this a few times and your girl knows how to find something to do, challenge her to do so without you, the family-camp activities director, the next time.

Anything with an on/off switch*

This is going to sound like the announcement we used to hear from the flight attendant when the plane was being pushed back from the gate, but do not be afraid to kindly insist that there are times when your family's electronic devices should be "powered down."

Before going any further, I have a secret to divulge. That flight attendant's reason for asking you to turn off your smartphone and take the ear buds out wasn't what she was telling you. These things have zero impact on the airplane's navigational equipment. No pilot in the history of aviation has radioed to the tower that he's experiencing some kind of interference from a passenger's electronics. Never.

So why did that nice person walk up and down the aisle like a hallway monitor in a grade school, making sure you're not sneaking one final text message . . . as though you'd ever do such a thing? The answer is going to make a lot of sense.

The airlines have their rule about electronic devices for the very reason you and I should have rules in our homes. These little suckers are a powerful distraction. And when the airplane you're on is getting ready to take off, the Federal Aviation Administration is telling you—without actually saying it so that passengers don't freak out—that this is the second most dangerous moment of your trip. The most dangerous is when your plane is making its "final approach" to the landing strip. And, of course, the rule about turning things off applies then as well.

What your flight attendant was saying is what we should be telling our family during certain times about these little devices.

"Right now, we need your full attention. This is no time to be checking your email or tweeting or sending an Instagram. Just in case we have something really important to say, we need to know that we have your eyes and ears."

You may have heard of Norman Rockwell. During my lifetime, he was the artist who captured moments in American life as no other artist ever had before. One of his most famous paintings, called "Saying Grace," is of a woman and a boy at a restaurant table. Their heads are bowed. The woman's hands are folded in front of her. There are two workmen—obviously strangers to the pair—also sitting at the table, gawking at the woman and the boy. Because there were no other seats available for lunch, they must have asked if they could sit there.

The young boy's back is to you and he's looking down. Although this painting was released in 1951, long before technology had made its way into our lives, the boy's pose looks very familiar. How could Mr. Rockwell have known?

Seriously, the kid is joining the woman and praying for the food, but it looks like he's sending a text message. See for yourself.[3] Even though you and I are smiling at the irony, it's not actually that funny because it's true. The distractions of our electronics are epic. The next time you're in a restaurant, look around. You'll see. Walk down the concourse of your airport or a busy sidewalk in a big city or the hallways of your local junior high. You'll see. Look at people everywhere, and they're gazing into their hands. You and I are doing the same thing. (In fact, your smartphone is probably within your reach right now. Yes?)

My advice may sound simplistic. Perhaps unrealistic, too. But please do everything you can as a dad to stay ahead of this. Be in charge—the gentleman security guard. Don't let those little screens get in the way. Please keep them from distracting you and your daughter so much that you stop looking at each other and listening carefully to every word spoken. Remember, listening is something you do with your eyes. Dare to set guidelines and keep them. Don't be brittle or brutal. Only remember that these wonderful gadgets were invented to serve us, not to enslave us.

Lying*

Like disobedience, lying can be a serious issue. A person who grows up not fully appreciating the importance of truth telling is a person bound to live a painful life. Let your daughter know that dishonesty is absolutely unacceptable.

As our girls were growing up, we had a policy about truthfulness that you and your wife may want to discuss before you make it a house rule. But if you do this, it will reward your daughter for telling the truth.

Here's the policy: There will be no punishment if you tell the truth the first time you're asked about what happened.

Of course, there may be unavoidable *consequences* for what your daughter has done—like having to ask a neighbor for forgiveness after hurting the little girl next door, or getting a failing grade after cheating on a test at school. But if the truth is told the first time, there will be no direct punishment—spanking or loss of privileges.

This accomplishes two important things. First, it ensures that the lines of communication between you and your girl will stay open. She will be rewarded for being truthful. (Isn't lying usually committed because of the fear of punishment? Then telling the truth ought to be rewarded.)

Second, because of the relationship you've established with your daughter through conversation, affection, and so forth, she will want to avoid disappointing you through misconduct.

In the New Testament, the apostle Paul reminded Christians in the city of Corinth that Christ's love for them ought to "compel" them (2 Corinthians 5:14). Other translations of that word include "constrain," "arrest," and "straighten out."

Your relationship with your daughter and your love for each other will naturally have an "arresting" and "straightening out" effect on her behavior. Don't be afraid that the no-punishment-for-the-truth rule will turn into reckless behavior. Your mutual love will provide plenty of control.

Manners*

Teaching your daughter good manners gives her a priceless gift that will last a lifetime. In chapter 4, we talked about the way to teach your daughter to greet adults: "It's nice to meet you, Dr. Holland." And as I mentioned, the payoff that she'll receive from Dr. Holland and other grown-ups will more than compensate her for her effort.

Table manners. We have friends who, like us, have two daughters. Every once in a while, maybe two or three times a year, they have a formal dinner at their own home—candles, the "good" china, classical music, the whole thing. They call it Going to the White House. And although it's treated like a game, it's a serious way of teaching their young girls how, when the time is appropriate, to act properly. Manners are not taught in most schools. If your girl doesn't learn everything from how to pass a plate to how to set the table at your house, she won't learn it. Always keep in mind that this is for her benefit, not yours.

"Yes, sir" and "Yes, ma'am." I know there will be an honest difference of opinion on this issue (like maybe you think I'm living during the Harding administration), but when Bobbie and I moved to the South, we noticed that some youngsters used "Sir" and "Ma'am" when addressing adults. We really liked the respect those terms communicated, so we asked that when the girls spoke to adults, including us, they would use "Sir" and "Ma'am." Because they were quite young, they had no trouble complying.

We made this decision because we felt that encouraging our girls to use those terms was an important symbol of respect. But using words that honored others also had an impact on our children's *self*-respect. Adults would invariably speak graciously to our daughters in response to being referred to as "Sir" or "Ma'am." Respect given was respect *received*, and respect *received* was respect *believed*.

In the classic movie and stage play *My Fair Lady*, Professor Henry Higgins changed Eliza Doolittle's life with a single thing: He changed the way she spoke. Teaching your daughter how to speak graciously and courteously will have the same impact.

Public-places manners. We broke "going out" into two categories: kid things and adult things. When we went out as a family or when it was a church social with lots of other families, that was a kid thing. At those times, it was not only acceptable to act like a kid, but it was also a requirement—have fun and enjoy yourself with the other children.

However, if the function was a "mostly adult" affair, like a wedding or church service, the order of the day was to act like an adult. In fact, when we would arrive at such events, I would say to the girls, "Look around. What kind of people do you see?"

They would reply, "Grown-ups."

Then I would say, "Okay, then how are we going to act?"

And the predictable—and correct—response was, "Like grown-ups."

What this primarily meant was that the girls stayed with their mother and me. The temptation was strong to run up and down the aisles after the service or to buzz through the hazelnuts on the punch-and-cookies table, but because this was an adult event, they didn't do those things. *Before* you arrive at these functions, be certain you have made your expectations clear.

Your level of resolve on these issues will keep this area of manners from becoming a battlefield. There's no need to be angry in verbalizing your expectations to your daughter. But she needs to realize that when you say, "This is the way we would like for you to act," that's exactly what you mean.

On your way home from extraserious and extralong adult events, when your daughter has been very good, tell her she acted like a princess. Then stop for frozen yogurt and let her have sprinkles on hers!

Messiness

Although it's true that no kid ever died of a messy room, the thing about living in a family is that one person's thoughtlessness will often affect someone else. We have friends who referred to leaving a mess, even in their own bedroom, as "smoke." They encouraged their children not to do it, since everyone else had to "smell" the messy person's "smoke," and that wasn't fair to the others.

Another dad told me that he asked his children to stop in the doorway and turn around before they walked out of a room. If someone walking into the room would be able to tell they had been there, they were asked to go back and "remove all evidence." This is a matter of common courtesy, and it helps to keep some order in your home.

Finishing homework

It has been a long time since you were in grade school. So you may have forgotten how fidgety and impatient you became at the end of the school day, anxious to get out of there.

Here is where you can begin to help your daughter with time management. Give her some time for herself right after school. Don't make her jump right into her homework. But before dinner, have her get some of it finished. Then, in the evening, she's not facing all of it without having gotten a head start.

If you think your girl has too much homework, talk to her teacher. You may find that your daughter isn't getting her work done at school. But if you discover that the teacher thinks she's still running her own PhD program at the university, respectfully encourage her to back off a little.

I have a good friend who visited his son's teacher. After learning that the teacher treated lots of homework like some sort of sacred rite, my friend said, "You have possession of my son for seven hours every day. I promise that I'll monitor my son in the evening, ensuring that he puts in one solid hour of homework a day. After that, he belongs to me."

Though that sounds reasonable and fair to me, try it at your own risk.

Selecting friends*

The impact of friends will be another seesaw in your daughter's life—with little effect when she's small, but growing to be fairly significant as she gets older.

You need to know who her friends are. As much as possible, have her friends come to *your* home. Doing this will give you a good idea of who these other children are and what kind of influence they might have on your girl.

Having other children to your house may be the only chance they'll have to see what a Christian home looks like. Imagine the impact your family could have on some youngster. This is how my wife came to the faith when she was eight years old—playing with a girl in the neighborhood, visiting her home, and discovering what it was like to live in a Christian home. This Christian family eventually led my wife's entire family to church and then to personal faith in Christ.

Second, talk to your daughter about her choice of friends, especially if some of those choices are creating some concern in you. This must be handled carefully, not because you don't have the right or are in some way afraid to discuss these issues, but because you want your daughter, as she grows up, to begin making her own sound friendship decisions. If you're making them for her, you're not teaching her anything except "What Dad says goes." That's not a helpful lesson for her to have learned, because when she's on her own, you won't be around to say anything. Then what will she do? That's right, make bad choices.

As you're discussing her friends with your daughter, do two important things:

1. Make "I" statements. Talk to your daughter about how *you* felt when you were around her friend. For example, "When you were playing with Ginger, it seemed to me that she was always taking things from the other children. Seeing a child who acts selfishly makes me very sad." Or "When I talked to Cindy, I noticed she said sassy things about her mother. Did you notice that?"

You're giving your daughter a chance to make the same observations you've made without feeling defensive. You're not saying, "You certainly do pick selfish, thoughtless friends to play with, don't you?" If you approach this delicate situation awkwardly, you'll have a battle on your hands. And you'll have earned it.

2. Ask questions. Once you've made certain observations, ask your daughter if she noticed the same things and how they made *her* feel. Listen carefully to her answers. What you're looking for is your girl's honest appraisal of this friend. If she shares some of your concerns, you may end the conversation with, "Do you think it might be a good idea for you to spend more time with your other friends and less time with Ginger or Cindy?"

Start this process as early as you can. Giving your daughter permission to honestly and openly discuss her friends with you when they're at the chalk-drawings-on-the-sidewalk stage will be a valuable bridge you can use when she's much older and the stakes are considerably higher.

Choosing and wearing clothes

Avoiding the temptation to put an asterisk next to this category, I will simply say that what your daughter wears is an important issue. Most girls, even if they're dressed in a way that communicates a disregard for what they look like, are *intentionally* dressed that way! But since I believe in the adage "You act as you are dressed," let me encourage you to do the following:

As much as you can, give her approved "choices." There will come an age—it may be as young as two or three years old—when your daughter will have strong opinions about what she wears. She'll resist you or your wife telling her exactly what to wear. So give her a choice. Lay out two, three, or four outfits, and tell her that she may "choose any of these."

That way, even though she feels as if she's being given a choice, you can't go wrong.

Avoid extremes. You don't want your daughter to get her identity from what she wears. Ultimately, you want her to be known by her character.

For a short time, Missy went to a private, all-girls school. Every student wore the same outfit, with absolutely no room for individual creativity. At first, I thought that would be a problem for our daughter, but in no time, she literally forgot about her clothing. It was *not* an issue. It also was a real frustration-saver every morning during the formerly traditional what-should-I-wear-today discussions (battles).

The goal is to encourage your daughter to wear the "uniform" of her school. That is, don't allow her to make her clothes either a source of embarrassment—because you've forced her into "out of it" clothes—or a source of identity—because you've allowed her to step out of line, either overdressing or underdressing. Normally, you're against the whole notion of conformity, but in this situation, let her be comfortable with her clothes. Let her be stylish but not extreme, matching what most of her classmates are wearing. Then she'll forget about it.

> *You have the right, even an obligation, to tell your daughter that something she's wearing could communicate the wrong thing to a boy.*

Encourage modesty. Here's where your experience as a man is your greatest asset. You have the right, even an obligation, to tell your daughter that something she's wearing could communicate the wrong thing to a boy. Most girls, it seems, have no idea about this. They may wear something provocative that they would call "cute." You can tell them that to a boy it's not cute; it's an absolute, jaw-dropping turn-on.

Although it's easy to notice only when your daughter is wearing something questionable, please be quick to tell her how wonderful she looks when she's wearing something conservative. An honest compliment from a male (you) will be highly motivating to her.

Selecting music

Can we skip this one? No? Okay, let's talk about it.

There are two legitimate and different concerns regarding music. The first is musical style. The second is musical message.

This may be tough for you and me to accept, but there is, by and large, no morality—or immorality—attached to particular musical styles. Rock is not immoral, and classical is not moral. Country is not immoral, and jazz is not moral.

Regardless of your or your daughter's particular taste, I encourage you to foster a *balance* of musical styles. Play a variety of music at your house. Take your girl to the symphony. When you're in the car together, let her choose the radio stations. If you can't stand it or you think you might be getting carsick, respectfully ask if it would be okay to change the music.

We did tell our girls that even though most musical styles are amoral, some music is more calming than other kinds. We said that if the girls "had" to go to sleep or wake up to music, classical was their only choice. We did some battle with this, but eventually we reached an agreement. (Again, good luck with this one.)

As you already know, musical *messages* can be immoral. Don't be afraid to ask your daughter what the words are, because you may not be able to tell what the singer is saying. She can tell. Ask her.

The greatest gift to you in this area is contemporary Christian music. Except for the extremes you find in mainstream music, there's enough variety in Christian musical styles to assuage any appetite. What will be missing will be the lyrics that promote things you don't believe in.

Handling money*

When was the last time you heard a dad complaining that his teenager "just doesn't appreciate the value of a dollar"? Yesterday? Me, too.

During the summer of 1967, when I was 19 years old, I cranked up my courage and asked a 21-year-old girl to dinner. Even though I was trying to save all my hard-earned money for my next college semester, I decided to take Jezebel (not her real name) to the most expensive restaurant in the area. When you're 19, you need to go the extra mile to impress an older woman.

Jezebel knew I was working to pay for school. On the way to dinner, I talked about how tough it was for me to earn enough during the summer to make a serious dent in tuition costs. But when the waitress came to take our order, Jezebel almost knocked me off my chair. She chose the most expensive entrée on the menu. In fact, there was a fine-print notation under the "Salads" section that read "Roquefort dressing, $1.00 additional." And Jezebel ordered the Roquefort dressing.

It was a short night. I had to report to the construction site early the next morning in order to put in a few extra hours to cover Jezebel's thoughtlessness. Later, I heard that the following semester she met a lovely guy named Ahab, and that was the last I heard of her. Good luck, Ahab.

You can start teaching your daughter about money and its value when she's quite young. Teach her that there are only three uses for money: spending, saving, and giving. Show her, by your own example, how this works and why each of these uses is important: Spending is for living today, saving is for living tomorrow, and giving is the best way for money to make everyone—giver *and* recipient—happy.

Show your girl how to be frugal. Order water when you're out to dinner. Restaurants put a huge markup on drinks, so let them do it on the backs of dads who haven't read this book. Make a game out of coupon shopping at the grocery store.

Help your daughter be creative in finding ways of making money. You can find books that will offer useful ideas. Once she has begun collecting money of her own, show her how much to spend, save, and give.

If you're in the kind of financial condition that makes it possible for you to give your daughter all the money she needs, be careful. Give her the joy of investing her own money in something important to her. You'll be amazed at how much more she'll appreciate the things she buys with her own money than the things she's given.

Not long ago, my friend George told me the story of his daughter's bicycle. My guess is that George and his wife would have been in a financial position to painlessly buy Ginger a bike. Instead, he and his daughter developed a plan whereby they would split the cost. He told her, "You come up with a hundred dollars, I'll match it, and we'll buy your bike." It wasn't easy, but Ginger worked and saved, and they bought the bike together. Actually, when George told me the story, he referred to this bike as "my daughter's immaculate bicycle." Any guesses why she takes that kind of care of her bike?

A year later, Ginger told her dad she'd like a special new tennis racket. When George and Ginger sat down to discuss the financial arrangements, Ginger finally told her dad to never mind. She'd use her mother's tennis racket!

If your family lives month to month and just keeps up with the bills, your daughter's active participation in the financial well-being of your family—as long as it's not overdone—will be a wonderful, character-building experience for her. Be sure you regularly express your gratitude for her help.

She'll understand at an early age what she'll need to know when she's married or on her own: the value of money. And because most American households depend on the woman to be the bookkeeper, you'll be giving your daughter's future family a wonderful gift.

Boys*

No single dating—one boy, one girl, one car—until she's at least 16. Group dates or going to a school or church function before 16 are okay. Then after her 16th birthday, just know who the boys are. (See chapter 3.)

Over the years, dads have asked me about this hard-and-fast 16-year-old rule. "Some girls are mature enough at 14, and some aren't ready until they're 18," they suggest. Of course, that's absolutely true. It's no different from our state "arbitrarily" deciding that at 16, your daughter is ready to drive a car or that at 18, she's ready to vote in a national election. Nonetheless, those are the laws.

My suggestion is that even if your daughter is mature enough to go out on a single date when she's 14, waiting two years won't inflict any permanent damage on her psyche. Make her wait. And if she's not ready at 16, don't push her into it. Let her wait until she's comfortable and, therefore, ready to tackle it on her own.

Perhaps the most frequent question I get on this subject is, "What if I just don't like the boy who wants to take out my daughter?"

If that's your question, please listen to what I'm about to say as carefully as you would if your life depended on it. First, you treat this boy's relationship with your daughter the same as you have any other friendship of hers from the time she was small. (See the "Selecting friends" section earlier in the chapter.) Your success in building a relationship with your daughter based on open conversation, affection, and discipline will serve you very, very well once boys begin to appear on the scene.

Second, the interviewing process will have a natural sifting effect on the universe of boys willing to meet with you before courting your daughter. As long as you remember that you are *not* interviewing to decide whether your daughter can or can't see this boy—every boy passes—the process itself will fix most of your unsuitability concerns.

Finally, your high level of involvement in your daughter's friendships will have a powerful influence for good in the lives of those young people. This way your daughter won't be the only positive influence in the lives of her friends who haven't had the luxury your girl has had—growing up with a dad like you!

Get involved in the process. This is not a spectator sport.

Curfew

Curfew time should not be a hard-and-fast rule. Every situation creates its own be-home-by times. Just be sure you've established that time and that she always calls or texts you if she can't make it by then. It may make you feel you're doing a good thing to require that your daughter always be the first one home out of her group of friends, but for her, it will become an unnecessary and counterproductive source of embarrassment. Don't die on this hill.

Smoking and alcohol

Rule number one is that there's no way you can enforce any guidelines here that are inconsistent with your own behavior. If you try it, she'll call your hand, and she has a right to.

I know that within Christian circles, there are honest differences of opinion regarding these issues, but let me take a run at them. Smoking is stupid. Ask anyone who smokes or has smoked. The vast majority of smokers will tell you they smoke for reasons other than the pure enjoyment of sucking blue smoke into their lungs. If your daughter starts to smoke, and this one's hard to hide, don't go crazy. Your overreaction will make the situation worse. Instead, talk to her. Listen to her. Pour on the verbal and physical affection. Talk to her in unemotional tones about the certainty of smoking's physical damage to her body.

If her smoking persists, you may want to find a Christian counselor who can help you discover ways to get through to your girl. (If you have no idea where to find a counselor in your area, I suggest visiting Focus on the Family's counseling-referral website at *http://www.focusonthe family.com/counseling/find-a-counselor.aspx* or calling 1-800-A-FAMILY. You can also arrange to speak with a licensed Christian counselor at no cost by calling 1-855-771-HELP (4357) Monday through Friday between 6:00 a.m. and 8:00 p.m. Mountain time.

Alcohol is about two things: the law and association. First, in every state, there are laws making underage drinking illegal. Don't allow your daughter to break those rules, even in your home. Second, alcohol and teenagers is about association—who they're hanging out with, peer pressure, and being cool.

Here's a case where "consequences" are your ally. Almost daily news reports will tell about people dying on the streets from using alcohol.

If you live in a big city, you'll find a story almost every day. If you live in a rural area, it may be once a month. In any case, make certain your daughter understands the potential perils of alcohol abuse.

Having said that, let me encourage you not to let alcohol be an issue that destroys your relationship. Find a balance. In too many Christian homes, this becomes a needless sticking point—a major source of conflict. Do everything you can to steer clear of this. Above all, talk about it without raising your voice. Don't give her a reason (like a dad who's unreasonable and inflexible) for escaping and drinking to excess.

And Finally . . .

Never stop working on yourself. The truth be known, you and I are constantly doing battle with appropriate versus inappropriate behavior. As you work on improving yourself, tell your daughter about the tough challenges you're facing. Your openness will give her permission to let you in on her own growing edges and allow you to provide encouragement and help.

Builder's Checklist

1. *Speak the "finished product" to your daughter.* By saying kind or complimentary things to your daughter or about other children in her presence, you can clearly communicate the value you place on certain qualities. Begin with the end in mind.
2. *Correct conduct is a by-product of other qualities you've built into your daughter.* Protection, conversation, affection, discipline, laughter, and faith should precede an emphasis on conduct.

3. *Make sure the guidelines for conduct are clearly defined.* Whatever they are, be certain that your daughter understands the rules. This is especially true for electronic gadgets. Don't surprise her with midcourse corrective "slaps." They won't work.

4. *Remember that communication is still the key.* Your ability to talk through conduct issues, explaining why you've decided to set certain guidelines, will help to keep your home free from outbreaks of hostility. Having said that, however, if you decide to hold the line on certain conduct-related issues, don't expect your daughter to applaud your every decision. And when she doesn't, that's okay.

PART THREE

Gentlemen, We Have Our Assignments

A Quick Look Inside

The Guy from the City Inspector's Office

What lies behind us and what lies before us are
tiny matters compared to what lies within us.
—Oliver Wendell Holmes

We've been talking about the ingredients necessary to build a daughter successfully. How well are you doing? You may only be starting with a tiny girl. You have almost everything to look forward to. Or you may be well on your way with a daughter who is growing tall and strong.

Let me ask you again, how well are you doing?

During the summers of 1966, 1967, and 1968, I worked for Richard Whitmer and Sons, a Chicago-area building contractor. Because Whitmer had decided that his would be a small company, I was his only full-time employee. The "and Sons" on the side of his truck only meant that he had two sons. Jim and Jerry loved their dad, but working for him in the construction business just wasn't going to happen.

When Whitmer landed large projects, he would bring in subcontractors to do the additional work. But for the most part, during those summers, it was just Dick Whitmer and me.

As an 18-year-old boy, working for Whitmer gave me a love for construction . . . and for Whitmer. And we (Dick, mostly) did it all—concrete pouring, masonry, framing, welding, electrical, plumbing, and trim work. I had never labored so hard in my life, but I experienced the thrill of working, finishing, and then standing back and actually seeing what I had helped to build. It was a feeling I never outgrew.

Of course, construction is filled with dangerous and even potentially deadly situations. Nearly every day, I'd do something to myself—bang my head on the scaffolding, drop a sheet of plywood on my foot, or skin my arm on something. Fortunately, I never did battle with any power tools. This didn't happen until I was well into my fifties.

When Dick would hear me say "Ouch!" or moan about something, he'd always ask if he could see it. It was probably an insurance-company requirement. I'd show him the injury, and he would say, "Hey, if it grows back, we don't worry about it." So much for compassion.

Of all the on-the-job injuries I had, I most hated getting wood splinters in my hands. Give me a sharp bang on the head with a protruding 2-by-10, but please, please don't give me a sliver. When Dick would ask to see it, I'd have to show him. Recognizing what I had buried in my tender finger, Dick would pull out his large and well-worn pocketknife, flip it open, "disinfect" it by wiping it across his work pants, and cut out the splinter. I had to tough it out like in the old cowboy movies, when a victim's compadres would remove a bullet from his leg. Sometimes tears would trickle down my cheek, but I'd never make a sound. I learned this so well that, even today, I have a hard time griping about things that hurt. However, at my age, this isn't necessarily a virtue. How many times have you heard about a guy who dropped dead of a heart attack when he had ample advanced warnings and just decided to push through the discomfort? Chest pains and bumps on your shin are not the same thing.

Someone Is Watching

So, with my introduction to the construction business, it was usually just the two of us on these building sites. I remember thinking, *How fun. Dick and I can do just about anything we want on the job. We can do work on this building, button the job up, and then get on with the next one . . . just like constructing a fort in the backyard with my friends, only much better.*

This was before I knew anything about building inspectors. Every city and county in America has them. Chicago, where I lived, had lots and lots of them. Their job is to visit construction sites and approve the contractor's work at the completion of every stage. The next time you visit an unfinished building, look for the building permit posted in a prominent place. You'll see the initials of the various inspectors who, by their approval, gave the contractor permission to move on to the next stage in the process.

If an inspector found something he didn't judge to be according to "code," or if he was just having a bad day, he would make us go back and fix the problem before going ahead. Those delays were not only frustrating, but according to Dick, they could also be extremely costly.

I came to deeply respect—and fear—the power of the building inspector.

WHO'S GOING TO INSPECT OUR WORK?

We started this book with an understanding that building a daughter is one of the most wonderful and challenging "projects" you and I will ever face. It's filled with lots of hard work, coupled with the joy of standing back to see what we've built. It also has its share of dangers—bumps, scrapes, and splinters—along the way.

God knows my work is a reflection of my character.

But who inspects *our* work? To whom do we answer for the quality of our performance?

A long time ago, King David wrote something sobering about the process of inspection:

Search me, God, and know my heart;
test me and know my anxious thoughts.
See if there is any offensive way in me,
and lead me in the way everlasting. (Psalm 139:23-24)

Did you catch *what* the Inspector is inspecting? He's not checking my work. He's inspecting *me*. God knows my work is a reflection of my character. If my heart meets "code," my work—as a person or a dad—will be acceptable to Him.

C'MON, YOU CAN SAY IT

In a sense, this chapter is a footnote, because instead of helping you with one more technique toward properly building your girl, it's about you and me—the builders.

Are you alone right now? If not, I want you to either clear the room or go somewhere by yourself. In chapter 2, we admitted, out loud, that we are quitters. Well, I've got another one. And since this is just between you and me, I don't want anyone else to hear you.

I want you to say the following at least loud enough so you can hear the sound of your own voice. I'm serious. In fact, while I'm writing this, I'll say it out loud too, so you won't be saying it all by yourself.

Are you ready? Is the room clear? Okay, say the following in an audible voice. No fair whispering.

"I need inspection."

Did you say it? Good.

Before you and I have a chance to be effective fathers, we have to become complete men. And before we can become complete men, we have to admit what we just admitted. We must admit that we're *not* complete, and we could use some regular internal inspection.

BEYOND TECHNIQUE AND STYLE

Here's a pretty sobering thought: Your success as a dad will have far more to do with who you are than with how well you're able to do certain things with and for your daughter. Ultimately, she will learn more by watching you than by listening to you—more from your example than from your teaching techniques.

This means you could be a perfect father "performer." You could understand your need to protect your daughter; you could be a brilliant conversationalist; you could learn to be a tender daddy and a tough disciplinarian; you could laugh with your girl; you could faithfully take her to church; and you could establish crystal-clear guidelines for conduct. You could do all these things and be a colossal failure.

The lesson is clear: As dads, with the principles we've just talked about, you and I may find ourselves attentive to visible tactics—to-do lists—for effective fathering. That's good. But if we forget that our true success will come only from what's inside our own hearts, we're destined for predictably heartbreaking consequences.

PLEASE, NO MORE LISTS!

One day, your girl will be grown and gone. She will have a life of her own and, except for occasional visits, calls, or text messages, her need for you will be near zero. This book has already given you more lists of things to do than you've ever seen in one place, so let me boil everything down to just a few final things you need to keep in mind in order to be ready for inspection. Without these, you could still be a terrific dad. But you'd be completely missing out.

1. Your personal walk with Christ. Only Jesus has the power to make dads complete. The apostle Paul said it this way: "In Him [Jesus Christ] you have been made complete" (Colossians 2:10, NASB).

Simple, isn't it? For you to be a complete man—and dad—Jesus Christ offers you the gift of completeness. Wholeness. Comfort. And He does this every day. From the sleepless nights when you first bring your daughter home to the terror you feel about turning her loose, God promises His wisdom and peace.

Begin your day with prayer. Find somewhere you can do this on your knees. Thank God for His goodness. Confess your sins. Pray for courage to think and do the right thing. Pray for your wife and your daughter. Ask God to make you His worthy representative in your workplace and to your family.

Read and study the Bible each day. This book is God's Word to you and me.

Several years ago a good friend told me about a phone call he had just received from a high school classmate named Gordon. It had been 20 years since they had spoken, so this call came from nowhere. Gordon started right in. "I just prayed, repented of my sins, and received Jesus Christ as my Savior."

My friend celebrated the good news but was shocked. This man, whom he remembered very well from high school as a cad and a bounder, had embraced salvation. But this ne'er-do-well rebel teenager had remembered my friend from high school and knew that he was a Christian. A kid who had lived for Jesus. So he found his number from a mutual friend and called him with the good news.

They talked for a long time, bringing each other up to date on what had happened over the years. "Do you have a Bible?" my friend finally inquired.

"Yes," the new convert replied. "I went to a Christian bookstore and bought one that the clerk recommended." Then his voice dropped. My friend had no idea why.

"What's the matter?" he asked.

"Have you seen this thing?" Gordon said. "It's huge!"

They both laughed.

"You're right," my friend returned. "But I can help you work your way through it."

If you're like this new convert and really don't have a sense of what the Bible is or how to work your way through it, here's a suggestion. A few years ago, R. C. Sproul and I wrote a book called *What's in the Bible?*[1] It's a sweeping overview of this daunting volume so you can see how it's organized and how to understand it.

There are also many wonderful Bible study books and guides available, but if you've never read the Bible, start with the Gospel of John. This is an account of the life of Jesus, written by His closest friend.

Pray and read your Bible every single day. Have a place that reminds you of your time alone with God—a quiet spot that becomes the special location for your private meeting.

2. Regular church attendance is a non-negotiable. Church attendance isn't something you and your daughter should need to haggle over week by week as she's growing up. Saying that may seem hardheaded and inflexible. Perhaps I am, but for good reason. Except for your home, there is no place on earth that's quite like the church. When you think about it, this eclectic gathering of folks who have willingly made their way to a common location is a wonder. An unexplainable phenomenon. People from all walks of life collecting themselves to do the same thing—to worship.

Bobbie has a friend whose college-age daughter, Sydney, was in full-blown rebellion. To say that she had dipped her toe into the waters of wandering and sin would be to greatly understate what was going on in this young woman's life. In her open recalcitrance, she had jumped completely into dark, turbulent waters, feetfirst.

When Sydney was home from college for a weekend, her mom

asked her if she would be willing to go to church, something they had done as a family all through the growing-up years. Surprisingly, her daughter said yes.

In the preprogam quietness, a familiar family—Steve and Linda Bennett and their three kids—slipped into the pew in front of Bobbie's friend, her husband, and Sydney. Linda Bennett was holding a sleeping infant whose skin color did not match the skin color of the rest of the family. Sydney saw the child and turned to her mother in astonishment. Her eyes widened.

"Did the Bennetts adopt a baby?" she whispered.

Her mom smiled and nodded.

"What kind of people would do something like this?" Sydney said, her whisper rising in volume to almost a speaking tone.

Bobbie's friend paused. She leaned over and whispered back to her daughter. "I guess . . . people who love Jesus."

The church service began, and there was no more conversation between Sydney and her mom. But they knew that they were both thinking about what they had just seen.

On the drive home, Sydney talked openly and with emotion about the family who had providentially chosen the seats in front of them in church that morning. She marveled at the kind of selfless love that would inspire a couple to do such a thing. To make this kind of sacrifice. Beyond her mother's simple explanation, Sydney had none.

In telling Bobbie about this moment in church, her friend had no other explanation for her daughter's recognition of her rebellion, her eventual confession to her parents of what she was doing with her life, and her resolve to turn away from the darkness. In the months—and, as it turned out, the years—that followed, Sydney changed. It was as though a light had been turned on that morning, sitting quietly in church, shedding its luster into the dark parts of Sydney's heart, showing her the radiant beauty of God's love. Who would ever have thought that such an innocent moment would have this kind of dramatic impact in a young woman's life? But it did.

Taking your daughter to church exposes her to the wonder of a God who draws people to Himself and then, by His transforming power, changes them in a way that cannot be hidden.

As your daughter grows up, why wouldn't church attendance with you be a non-negotiable?

3. *Someone to walk with you.* Many years ago, I had a long and wonderfully memorable conversation with a friend who had spent a lifetime as a psychologist and marriage therapist. He told me that when a new client comes to him, he always makes the same request in their first session: "Tell me about your three closest friends."

If the new client is a woman, the answer is usually quick in coming. Often, the woman will describe more than three friends and then explain how difficult it is to narrow the list to just three.

> *Find a group of friends, men to whom you can be regularly answerable for each of the key areas of your life.*

If the new client is a man, there's often a long pause, followed by the question, "What exactly do you mean by *closest* friends?"

Let's face it: Most men aren't adept at building close friendships. Sure, there are guys that you and I enjoy being with, golfing, watching the playoffs with, hunting or fishing with . . . but "close" friends? What exactly do I mean by close friends?

In his landmark best seller *The Man in the Mirror*, Patrick Morley said it this way: "God's Word teaches us how to stand firm in the faith and to guard against falling away. . . . Yet, men *do* fall away because they don't have to answer to anyone for their behavior and beliefs. . . . The answer—the missing link—is accountability."[2]

Find a group of friends, men to whom you can be regularly answerable for each of the key areas of your life. Don't try to go it alone.

In his book, Morley tells the story of Lawrence Taylor, the New York Giants linebacker who, in his prime, was one of the most skillful and ferocious the game had ever seen. But in 1988, after being suspended by the National Football League for violating its substance-abuse policy, Taylor was quoted in *The New York Times*:

> God, I didn't mean for it to happen. . . . I wish it hadn't,
> but I did make a bad decision and I'll pay the price for
> it. . . . I really wasn't allowing the Giants to help me. I wasn't
> allowing my wife to help me. I was doing it by myself and
> trying to make it happen by myself because I wanted to
> say I could do it on my own. It don't work like that. Boy, I
> found that out.

Find a few men—three to five—who would be willing to meet with you *regularly*. Commit to total honesty and confidentiality. Tell each other about the victories and the defeats in your personal life, your family life, and your work life.

In the book of Proverbs, King Solomon reminds us that

> As iron sharpens iron,
> so one person sharpens another. (27:17)

Allow other men to sharpen you as a man, a husband, and a dad.

Read books as a group—*The Man in the Mirror* would be a great one to start with. And pray together:

> Confess your sins to each other and pray for each other so
> that you may be healed. The prayer of a righteous person is
> powerful and effective. (James 5:16)

If the group is small enough for mutual conversation and trustworthy enough for honesty, this can be your lifeline to self-examination.

Several years ago when the news came of a Christian leader who had fallen into infidelity, a good friend of mine sent an emergency text message to his senior colleagues and ordered them to his conference room. As the CEO, he had the authority to do such a thing, and the response from his leadership team was predictable. In minutes they were all there, seated nervously around the table.

My friend thanked them for coming (like they had a choice, right?) and then told them why they were there. He told them about the fall of a person they all knew and how this news had personally rocked him. Then he looked around the table and spoke to each person by name, one at a time.

"Steve," he started with the first unlucky guy to his right. "You know how much I appreciate you. We've been working together for a lot of years, and I have trusted you to speak truth. But I have a question for you."

My friend's eyes were squarely on Steve's eyes. Neither one—especially Steve—blinked.

"Are you hiding anything, Steve? Is there something in your life that, if disclosed, could ruin everything—this business, your family . . . you?"

The room grew painfully quiet. Yes, my friend was speaking to Steve, but each man around the table knew his turn was coming.

You may be surprised when I tell you that my friend in this story is the pastor of a very large and prominent church. Most of the men around the table were ordained ministers. But in telling me this story, his eyes filled with tears. Some of the people on his staff were covering up. Things like excessive drinking and gambling and pornography were confessed. Since no one had loved them enough to go point-blank with them, they had been getting away with their secrets. The meeting lasted for several hours. And it closed with my friend confessing that he had been afraid to have a conversation like this with the men he trusted most. But he promised that from now on, transparency would rule the day and that meetings like this—where church business was set aside and each man was challenged to "live what he was preaching"—would become regular fare.

My friend told me that this meeting radically changed the course of their church. It's the power of accountability.

You and I cannot afford the luxury of living without this kind of accountability.

If you maintain a daily time with God, and if you join a church in your community where the minister holds the truth of the Bible in high regard and preaches from it, and finally, if you commit yourself to mutual transparency with a handful of friends, I can promise your life will be inspectable. And because of God's grace and mercy, you'll "pass code," ready to move ahead with the big job of successfully building your daughter into a well-balanced, godly, and complete woman.

Hey, good news! I just checked your "building permit," and God's signature is on it.

Builder's Checklist

1. *Prepare for inspection.* Every construction project—and man—has to face inspection.
2. *Watch your example.* Success in building a daughter is more dependent on your own life than on your ability to follow fathering techniques.
3. *Tend to your insides.* A dad's inner growth must include time spent alone with God.
4. *Join a local church.* Both you and your daughter need an extended family where you can meet and enjoy the friendship of other Christians. A place where you can learn and grow and rest in the fellowship of kindred spirits.

5. *Establish accountability.* Joining with a small group of friends, meeting to be accountable to one another, may be the most important thing you can do to stay on track as an effective father.

6. *Say the following prayer.* If you feel you need to recommit yourself to "being" rather than just "doing," you're welcome to pray the following prayer:

Dear God,
I admit that without You, my life doesn't pass Your code. But I
thank You for Your grace. I thank You that through Your mercy,
I have a way to pass Your inspection. I renew my commitment to
You as my Lord and Savior, and I promise never to forget that
from this moment on, I can tackle the job of building my daughter
with the strength of Your love and power. In Jesus's name, amen.

A CHAPTER FOR "SPECIAL" DADS

Stepdads, Long-Distance Dads, and Single Dads

During the summer of 1995, I was having breakfast with a new friend. Skip and I had met at church, and he was telling me the story of his life. I was filling him in on mine. When I told him I was writing a book for dads, he asked me an important question: "What are you saying to dads in special situations like mine—blended-family dads, stepdads, adoptive dads, or single dads?"

My first thought was that most of this book ought to fit regardless of a dad's particular situation, but I promised I would go back and carefully read it through one more time, just to be sure. Then, as an afterthought, I suggested that perhaps I should ask Skip, and a few other dads who are in one of those special situations, to review the manuscript and meet together to discuss it. So that's what we did.

The men met at my house, and we had a lively conversation about this book and what should be added for dads in special family situations. I was very grateful for their help.

BLENDED-FAMILY DADS

If your family includes your wife's daughter, the most critical issue you'll face is earning the right to *be* the dad. This girl is not your own, and she'll believe that she has the choice to obey you or not. "You're not my dad" will bring discussions, especially confrontational situations, to a speedy and painful end.

There's only one person who can give you official "permission" to be the dad, and that's the girl's mother—your wife. That means you and she need to regularly confer on issues related to your daughter and agree on specific strategies. All this must happen before you reveal those policies to your stepdaughter, so that when you do, your wife will back you up.

If your stepdaughter joined your family at age 12 or 13, you may need to ask your wife to take part in some of the fathering chores. For example, if you choose to interview boys (chapter 3) prior to your stepdaughter's going out on a date, your wife will probably need to do it, either alone or with you. She has the most history with her daughter, so she may need to take the lead.

Help your wife to understand that as she interacts with her daughter alone, her support of you will make or break your ability to be the dad—or one of the dads—for this girl.

One of the dads told us that through years of broken promises and neglect, his stepdaughter had learned to mistrust her biological father. What her father *said* had no bearing on what he *did* or how he lived. Through years of trustworthiness, my friend had just begun to win this girl's trust. He stressed the importance of patience and understanding.

Just a temporary bridge

Are you familiar with the temporary, floating bridges the military often uses to span a river quickly? Unlike permanent bridges made with lots of steel and concrete, these connections between two riverbanks can be assembled in a matter of hours.

However, unlike permanent spans, temporary bridges are more susceptible to destruction; raging rivers or guerrilla attacks can render them useless in a short time.

The relationship "bridge" between you and your stepdaughter is *not* a permanent bridge. When your family was blended and she came along with the deal, it happened relatively quickly. You weren't there when she was born. You didn't change her diapers or teach her to walk. One day she wasn't there; the next she appeared.

This relationship is temporary. Like the military bridge, it can be easily broken. You must remember that yesterday's passable bridge will not necessarily be there tomorrow. To ensure a safe crossing, through gentleness and humility on your part, the relationship will need constant maintenance.

How old is she?

The younger your stepdaughter was when she came to live with you, the more your relationship with her will be similar to dealing with your own child. The older she is, the more careful and deliberate you'll need to be.

Conversation is still the key. Talk to her—a lot. Text message her with simple notes that don't require a response. And don't overdo this. If you do, she'll feel pressure to do the same back to you. Gently let this girl know what's up in your life and give her a chance to reciprocate. Don't force this by interrogating her; instead invite her to be open by being gentle and willing to talk about your own challenges. As she reaches her teenage years, let her in on your ideas about being a dad—the whys and the strategies. If they make sense to her, ask her for the green light to be her coach and hold her accountable. Help *her* to paint the picture of the "finished product." If you do this, she'll be more open to your protection and discipline.

Careful affection

After reading this manuscript, one of the dads expressed his concerns related to affection (chapter 5), especially as his girl changed from being a child into a woman. He told our group that he has two daughters in his home, one a stepdaughter and the other his biological child. He told us how much he loves both girls, but he expressed the subtle differences between them. In every girl's life, there will come a time when she becomes aware of her own need for modesty around her dad. This time will likely arrive sooner with your stepdaughter than with your biological daughter. Honor her need for privacy.

He went on to tell us that most of the principles in *She Calls Me Daddy* were appropriate for both his daughters, but then he gave the following caution: "When it comes to physical affection, I'm more cautious with my stepdaughter. Somehow in the deepest recess of my heart, I *know* she's not my child. So I'm more careful physically. I'm very open with my verbal affection, but I let her take the lead with bear hugs and kisses."

Her other dad

Every blended-family situation has its own special conditions. Yours is no exception. If you're comfortable speaking to your stepdaughter's biological dad, I encourage you to make occasional contact, even by phone. Such calls can be important, especially as they relate to the task of effectively fathering this girl. Honor him by letting him know you want his input. However, don't do this without the full knowledge and consent of your wife and daughter. This is about cooperation, not conspiracy.

You may even suggest that her biological dad read this book, giving the two of you a basis for discussing specific ideas and approaches. The more you eliminate the opportunities for your girl to "play both ends against the middle," the more effective you'll both be. And the more you can contribute to a good relationship between your stepdaughter and her biological father, the healthier she'll be.

A volunteer dad and daughter

My first job right out of college was in full-time youth work. For seven years, Bobbie and I got to know hundreds of high schoolers. One thing that struck me early on was that all the kids we worked with *chose* to be involved in our club meetings and camps. They were all free agents, volunteers. When they wanted to meet with us, they did. But the moment they didn't want to be part of our program, they left.

I couldn't afford to make any assumptions about those relationships. I couldn't take the kids for granted. I had to constantly earn the right to be involved in their lives.

It's been almost 50 years since we first met some of those teenagers. They've grown up. Lots of them have families of their own. But as we've stayed in contact with some of them, we've come to realize that we were able to do this because we weren't coaches, parents, teachers, or ministers. The kids weren't players, children, students, or parishioners. We were all volunteers—the teenagers and us. We chose to be connected to each other.

Your role as a stepdad will be a lot like that. You have chosen to love this girl, and your hope is that she'll choose to love you, too.

LONG-DISTANCE DADS

One of the dads in our book review group was his daughter's biological father, but she lived with her mother in another city. He told us how painful it was not to have regular contact with her, and how he missed seeing her every day. The most significant thing he emphasized was the need for regular word touchings.

When Bobbie and I were falling in love, we had what we thought was a real problem. She lived in Washington, DC, and I was at school in Indiana. How could we possibly build this relationship when we lived so far apart?

Now, looking back on that time, we're both grateful for the distance. Was it *better* than being together? Probably not. But the miles gave us the chance to slowly but surely introduce each other to our deepest thoughts and feelings—in writing.

If you're a long-distance dad, even though you don't have the luxury of physically hugging your daughter every day, touch her with your words regularly. Spontaneous text messages with just a few words help maintain that contact.

I have a friend who tries to send a short email each day to his daughter. His notes may be mostly news, like: "The meeting with the Acme vice president went great. I think we might get the order. It would sure help me make my sales quota. I love you and I miss you, Amy. Love, Dad."

Her response may be as simple as "I've had a wild day—two tests and a paper—and I'm about to go to bed, but I just wanted to tell you I love you, Dad. Love, Amy."

These (almost) daily word touchings don't need to be filled with mushy things. Just provide regular updates to keep your daughter appraised. And every once in a while, shoot her a joke or a cartoon you found in the paper. Laughing together isn't as fun long distance as it is when you're together, but it can still help to seal the bond.

Although the bridge between you and your long-distance daughter is probably more permanent than the military span I talked about earlier with stepdads, there are times when it won't feel that way. But you can do something to keep the bridge strong, and you've got to do it constantly: Communicate!

Suck it up

Be careful with the things you tell your daughter about what's going on between you and her mother. One of the dads in our group summed up what he does when he's talking to his daughter about her mother: "I refuse to get involved in negative conversation about my ex-wife. I tell myself, *Bob, don't do this. It will not help your daughter to get caught in the middle. You might think you have the right to slam your ex, but don't do it. It won't help a thing. Just suck it up.*"

In fact, as much as you can, affirm your daughter's relationship with her mother. In most cases, your girl will be better for it.

Single Dads

You have a tough job. Never having been a young girl yourself, there will be times when you're mystified by what's going on with your daughter. If you've been widowed and you really *are* doing this fathering thing alone, pray for adult women who will befriend your girl. Church is the best place to find such women: the wife of the

Speak kind words about your ex-wife in your daughter's presence.

youth director, the mother of a friend your daughter meets, a Sunday school teacher. These women will save your life.

If you're divorced, encourage your daughter to build a solid relationship with her mother. Speak kind words about your ex-wife in your daughter's presence. This is the only mother your girl has, and if you can enhance their relationship, do it.

Lighten up

As a single dad, you may be tempted to lean too heavily on your daughter emotionally. Be careful. Resist the temptation to use her to meet your own relational needs. Don't force her to grow up too quickly just because you don't have an adult companion at the moment. Find a small group of men to walk through this with you. (See chapter 10.) They'll be a big help.

It's Never Too Late

Many "special" dads live with regrets. If you're one of those dads, you know that dwelling on the "if-only's" can bury you. Yes, you've made some choices that have unalterably affected your role as your daughter's daddy. This isn't how you expected your life to turn out.

However, let me encourage you to spend less time looking back and more time looking ahead. Someone has described the past as hardened concrete and the future as wet cement. Rather than filling your mind with what you could have or should have done, focus on what you can do from this point on.

Tell your daughter you're sorry about how your decisions have made her young years more of a challenge. But promise her that starting now, you want to recommit yourself to being the best dad—step, long-distance, or single—you can possibly be.

It's *never* too late to start being a better daddy.

QUESTIONS FOR DISCUSSION

Chapter 1

1. *Now, that's funny.* The book opens with a story about a Jockey-shorts-clad Robert getting caught at midnight in the living room by his daughter's friend. What funny story can you remember about your fathering experience? If your daughter is too young for you to have any funny stories yet, can you remember one from your own childhood?

2. *What gets you out of bed on a Saturday morning?* You may not be into building projects, but what would get you up early on a Saturday morning? Can you identify with how motivating it feels to look forward to something you really enjoy doing?

3. *The big day.* Recall the events leading up to and including the birth of your daughter. Did you want a girl, or were you a little—or a lot—disappointed that she wasn't a boy? Why?

4. *This particular project.* Why are you reading this book? Take a moment to reflect on what you would like to accomplish by spending some time reading and thinking about your relationship with your daughter. Are there any specific goals you'd like to set?

5. *You're the only daddy she'll ever have.* How does it make you feel to read that statement? Why?

Chapter 2

1. *Underestimating.* Remember a time when you underestimated how long something was going to take to finish. Did you

complete the project? If so, what got you through to the end? What project do you have going on right now that needs to get finished?

2. *Fessing up.* When was the last time you were so exasperated with your daughter that you felt like quitting?

3. *Not quitting.* Recall a situation when you were tempted to quit, but you finished instead. How did it feel when you didn't give in to the temptation?

Chapter 3

1. *Protection equals value.* Besides family and friends, name several of your things that you consider valuable. What measures do you take to protect them?

2. *The seesaw.* Explain the way physical and emotional protection change during your daughter's lifetime. Where is your daughter today regarding her need for each? Does she need a lot of protection or just a little?

3. *What's stopping you?* What keeps you from effectively carrying out your duty to protect your daughter? Why?

4. *Balance.* What are some examples where a dad's protection of his daughter could be overdone? Underdone? What can you do to strike a balance?

5. *The interview.* What is the purpose of interviewing your daughter's dates when she turns 16?

Chapter 4

1. *Powerful trouble.* Recall a situation when your words got you in trouble.

2. *Teaching conversation.* What benefits accrue to your daughter when you teach her how to carry on a conversation with you? With other adults? With boys? Why can text messages be a poor substitute?

3. *Getting started.* Given the current age of your daughter, what kinds of things could you do this week to improve her conversation skills?

4. *Crown jewel?* Why do you think Robert referred to conversation as the "crown jewel"?

Chapter 5

1. *Physical affection.* What are some examples of nondramatic but still meaningful touchings? What can you do with your daughter—what kinds of games could you play, for example—to increase the frequency of physical contact?

2. *Verbal affection.* Recall from your own childhood the memory of someone who spoke kind words to you. How do you feel about that person today? What are some moments you could capture to verbally touch your daughter?

3. *More deposits, please.* What can you do to improve the balance in your daughter's Love Bank account?

Chapter 6

1. *All yeses.* How does our culture promote the idea that yes is always good and no is always bad?

2. *Punishment.* How were you punished as a child? Who did the punishing?

3. *Swift, painful, and fair discipline.* Do you agree that discipline should be swift, painful, and fair? Why or why not?

4. *Discipline is its own reward.* What does this statement mean to you? How could it be applied to your own experience as a person in addition to your role as a dad?

Chapter 7

1. *The Sea Cloud Sport Boat.* When have you been hoodwinked by a certain expectation, only to find the reality far different?

2. *Laughing on purpose.* Is there enough laughter in your home? What do you do to bring laughter into your daughter's life?

3. *A little candor.* Are you fun to live with? On a scale of 1 (total bore) to 10 (wild and crazy guy), what number would you give yourself? Why?

4. *A little more candor.* On the same scale of 1 to 10, what score would your daughter give you? Why?

Chapter 8

1. *Take some time.* Go back over the list of ways to build godly character in your daughter from the Builder's Checklist at the end of the chapter.

2. *Check them out.* Which of the things on the checklist have you already done? Which would you like to start doing? What things would you add to the list?

3. *Goals to shoot for.* This list should be the foundation of a faith-building strategy for you and your daughter. Don't be overwhelmed by the size of the list; just pick a few goals and see how much fun this can be.

Chapter 9

1. *Your experience.* What kind of discipline did you receive as a child? How do you feel about it now? Why?

2. *Order?* Do you agree or disagree with Robert's reasons for putting this chapter at the end of the list of seven things to do as a father? Why?

3. *By-product.* What are some examples of how "fixing" something you're dealing with related to an earlier chapter could solve a conduct problem?

4. *Finished product.* How can you speak to the goal you're attempting to reach with your daughter? What kinds of things

could you begin doing right away to "paint this picture" for your girl?

5. *Unusual allies.* How can negative consequences and positive rewards be good helpers in your task of teaching your daughter proper conduct?

6. *What do you think?* As you review the list of issues related to conduct, ask yourself these questions: What do I agree with? What do I disagree with? Why?

7. *Work to do.* Based on your answers to the previous question, what do you need to begin working on with your daughter?

8. *Being liked is not as important as doing what's right.* How do you feel about this statement? How would it help you when the going gets tough with your daughter?

Chapter 10

1. *Building codes.* How might a community look if there were no building codes? Are you glad—even if you're a contractor!—for inspectors and codes? Why or why not?

2. *Your example.* In your own words, why does your ability as a father depend more on who you are than on how you employ certain fathering techniques?

3. *Your time of quiet reflection and prayer.* How are you doing in the disciplines of quiet times and prayer? How involved are you at your church? How can you sharpen this area of your personal life?

4. *To whom do you answer?* Do you have an accountability group? If not, list three men you think might be interested in doing this with you. Then call them and set up a meeting.

ACKNOWLEDGMENTS

There's nothing a man has that hasn't been given to him. I know this because I'm such a man.

My parents, Sam and Grace Wolgemuth, made me the envy of nearly all my friends. "I just love your parents" is something I've heard from the time I was a small boy right up to the present. Together they represented absolute toughness, tenderness, and godliness.

This book never would have been possible without Bobbie, the wife of my youth. Her love gave me the ability to believe in myself. Her creativity, laughter, and wisdom became the substance of our home. And her friendship and encouragement give me a boatload of anticipation for tomorrow's adventures.

The influence of my five siblings—Ruth, Sam, Ken, Debbie, and Dan—helped to shape me before I knew it. Their love and support today are as accessible as almost daily text messages of encouragement. Their spouses and children—and their children—are also very special to me. I am thankful for each one.

I deeply appreciate the tender relationship Bobbie had with her dad, Dr. Ray Gardner, who slipped quietly into heaven during the summer of 2013 as I was working on this manuscript. Bobbie's early relationship with her dad gave her the tools to trust me and enthusiastically support my connection with our daughters.

Our daughters, Missy and Julie, have hung in with their amateur dad from the time he made his first mistake with them until now. I am ever grateful for their patience during the early years and for their friendship today as grown-ups.

I'm thankful, too, for our sons-in-law, Jon Schrader and Christopher Tassy, gifts to our daughters. And God has blessed Jon with Abigail Grace and Christopher with Harper Corin and Ella Patrice. The fun of being the father of a daughter continues to the next generation. These men were a huge help in repurposing this book from its original publication in 1996; their advice and input were tremendous. I have loved watching them be such good daddies to their daughters.

I am thankful for the power of the gospel of Jesus Christ. Apart from His grace, I would be a miserable man . . . and would have been a treacherous father. I am humbled by His kindness to me and thankful for the chance to put some of my ideas and musings into a book—one that anyone would actually read and take to heart.

So, finally, I am grateful for you and the hours that we have invested in each other through the pages of this book. God's richest blessing to you.

GRACE WOLGEMUTH'S 26 BIBLE VERSES

A   All we like sheep have gone astray.—Isaiah 53:6

B   Be kind one to another.—Ephesians 4:32

C   Children obey your parents, for this is the right thing to do.—Ephesians 6:1

D   Don't fret or worry; it only leads to harm.—Psalm 37:8b

E   Every good and perfect gift is from above.—James 1:17

F   "Follow me," Jesus said, "and I will make you fishers of men."—Matthew 4:19

G   God is love.—1 John 4:16

H   He cares for you.—1 Peter 5:7

I   "I am the bread of life."—John 6:35

J   Jesus said, "Let the little children come to me." —Matthew 19:14

K   Kind words are like honey, enjoyable and healthful. —Proverbs 16:24

L   Love one another.—John 13:34

M   "My sheep hear My voice, I know them, and they follow Me."—John 10:27

N   Now is the time to come to Jesus.—2 Corinthians 6:2

O   Obey God because you are His children.—1 Peter 1:14

P   Pray about everything.—Philippians 4:6

Q   Quick, Lord, answer me, for I have prayed.—Psalm 141:1

R   Remember your Creator now, while you are young.
—Ecclesiastes 12:1

S   Sing a new song to the Lord.—Psalm 98:1

T   Thank God for Jesus, His gift too wonderful for words.
—2 Corinthians 9:15

U   Underneath are God's everlasting arms.—Deuteronomy 33:27

V   Visit the sick and fatherless.—James 1:27

W   We love because God first loved us.—1 John 4:19

X   Except a kernel of wheat fall into the ground and die, it
remains a single seed. But if it dies, it produces many seeds.
—John 12:24

Y   You must be born again.—John 3:7

Z   "Zacchaeus, you come down; for I'm going to your house
today."—Luke 19:5

Notes

Preface

1. A complete description of the ceremony can be found in *She Still Calls Me Daddy: Building a New Relationship with Your Daughter After You Walk Her Down the Aisle*. You may want to wait until your daughter is a lot older before you read that book.

Introduction

1. Actually, Bobbie did not join us at the Ballantyne. She stayed with our five grandchildren, at the time ranging in age from 10 to 17. They had even more fun than we did.

Chapter 1

1. Because my daughters were born in the Dark Ages, I was not allowed to cut the cord. Back then, no amateur was going to do such an important medical thing. In fact, Bobbie gave birth in a Roman Catholic hospital where the nurses shushed me out every time they came to examine her. I wanted to tell them that it was okay; I had seen my wife naked before. But I didn't have the courage to say this to a celibate nun, so I did as asked and exited the room.

2. Although you really shouldn't read it yet, some day you may want to get a copy of the sequel to this book, *She Still Calls Me Daddy: Building a New Relationship with Your Daughter After You Walk Her Down the Aisle* (Thomas Nelson, 2009).

Chapter 2

1. This balloon release happened years before concerns arose regarding the potential negative environmental implications of balloon releasing.

2. This was before the NFL added to their rule book a serious penalty for "spearing." Bill Bates could have been the inspiration for this rule.

3. Heroes? Yes. Isn't it ironic that both Reggie and Bill were outspoken about their love for Jesus?

Chapter 3

1. The danger of even mentioning technology in a book is that by the time this manuscript is complete and off to the printer, everything I have said about technology will be obsolete. Nonetheless, what's happening with electronically accessible information must be addressed.

Chapter 4

1. This doesn't count the over 200 million people in the United States who drive in cars every day. It also doesn't include buses or bicycles or ferries—mostly for the purpose of going to see someone else in person.

Chapter 5

1. In the next chapter, Adam gives her a formal name so she can print it on her stationery: "Eve."

2. Genesis 2:24

3. Genesis 3:3

4. Genesis 2:17

5. Julie spent her first few years in regular physical therapy, walking on time but with a limp. Although her leg never fully recovered, she underwent tendon transfer surgery when

she was 12. As an adult, she walks with a barely discernable hitch in her gait.

Chapter 6

1. This metaphor appeared in the first edition of this book in 1996. At that point, I had not personally experienced a kidney stone. But in 2005, I did. As you may know, this is nothing to joke about. Yikes.
2. If it's January and you live in Billings or Duluth or Bangor, my sincere apologies.

Chapter 7

1. http://goo.gl/wTsjDK

Chapter 8

1. Ephesians 6:4
2. The same is true, of course, if you have a son.
3. Genesis 2:21-24
4. Matthew 16:18, emphasis added
5. Many churches have wonderful programs for little kids. When you walk into the area designated for children, the decor shouts of Disneyland. This is wonderful. However, every once in a while, bring her to "big church" with you. Just like taking her along on your weekend excursions to the Home Depot, she'll have a chance to sit next to her daddy and experience something from your world—in this case, worship. She will be right next to you, so she will hear you sing and follow along in your Bible . . . or your smartphone or on your tablet. Because her attention span is a little shorter than yours, you will want to bring along something for her to do that doesn't make any noise. Paper for drawing is always a good choice. (Although I cannot give any theological reason for what I'm about to say,

I don't recommend that you let her use your phone or tablet during the sermon.) Then she'll not feel obligated to pay
special attention to your pastor's sermon series on the Minor
Prophets. She'll have her own activity to occupy the time.

6. From *The Book of Order of the Evangelical Presbyterian Church*,
© 2013, page 114.

7. If you search "teaching your child to pray" on your favorite
bookselling website, you'll see that there are many books from
which you can choose. You may also want to ask someone at
your church who specializes in kids' ministry.

8. Naming this particular cereal is for illustration and a smile
only. According to research, Honey Smacks (Sugar Smacks
when our kids were small) contains 57 percent sugar. Yikes.

9. These hymns and 45 more can be found on *Hymns for a Kid's
Heart*, © 2003, 2004, 2005, 2006 by Joni Eareckson Tada
and Bobbie Wolgemuth, various publishers.

10. All 26 verses are listed on pages 223–224.

11. When you use a search engine to look up "photos of the
universe," you will not believe what you'll see. Show these to
your daughter. Tell her that God did this.

Chapter 9

1. Every year over 40 million people agree.
2. See http://goo.gl/uM6nD
3. http://goo.gl/lbMpOE

Chapter 10

1. Sproul, R. C. and Wolgemuth, Robert. *What's in the Bible?*
Nashville: Thomas Nelson Publishers, 2011.

2. Morley, Patrick. *The Man in the Mirror*. Grand Rapids:
Zondervan, 1989.

FOCUS ON THE FAMILY®

Welcome to the Family

Whether you purchased this book, borrowed it, or received it as a gift, thanks for reading it! This is just one of many insightful, biblically based resources that Focus on the Family produces for people in all stages of life.

Focus is a global Christian ministry dedicated to helping families thrive as they celebrate and cultivate God's design for marriage and experience the adventure of parenthood. Our outreach exists to support individuals and families in the joys and challenges they face, and to equip and empower them to be the best they can be.

Through our many media outlets, we offer help and hope, promote moral values and share the life-changing message of Jesus Christ with people around the world.

Focus on the Family
MAGAZINES

These faith-building, character-developing publications address the interests, issues, concerns, and challenges faced by every member of your family from preschool through the senior years.

For More
INFORMATION

 ONLINE:
Log on to
FocusOnTheFamily.com
In Canada, log on to
FocusOnTheFamily.ca

 PHONE:
Call toll-free:
800-A-FAMILY
(232-6459)
In Canada, call toll-free:
800-661-9800

THRIVING FAMILY®
Marriage & Parenting

FOCUS ON THE FAMILY CLUBHOUSE JR.®
Ages 4 to 8

FOCUS ON THE FAMILY CLUBHOUSE®
Ages 8 to 12

FOCUS ON THE FAMILY CITIZEN®
U.S. news issues

Rev. 3/11

The Family project™
A Divine Reflection